Acting &
Directing

THIRD EDITION

Acting & Directing

Russell J. Grandstaff
Western Michigan University

National Textbook Company
NTC a division of *NTC Publishing Group* • Lincolnwood, Illinois USA

Cover photo courtesy of
The O'Malley Theatre of Roosevelt University

DIRECTOR: Yolanda Lyon Miller

SET DESIGNER: Robert Martin

ACTORS: Thad Mayhugh
Steve Kuhn
Marji Dainty
Elizabeth Pratt

(Scene from *A Midsummer Night's Dream*)

1993 Printing

Published by National Textbook Company, a division of NTC Publishing Group.
© 1990 by NTC Publishing Group, 4255 West Touhy Avenue,
Lincolnwood (Chicago), Illinois 60646-1975 U.S.A.
Manufactured in the United States of America.
Library of Congress Catalog Card Number: 88-60943

  2 3 4 5 6 7 8 9 ML 9 8 7 6 5 4 3

Contents

Introduction

Designed for beginning theatre students, this revised edition of *Acting & Directing* provides practical guidelines. Many individuals contribute to every theatre production, but only the actors and director work intensely together over a long period of time. The material covered here will assist you in recognizing the roles, responsibilities, and interrelationships of the actor and the director. It also will provide you with a background to appreciate the work of other artists of the theatre.

Theatre is a cooperative effort. No participant can operate in isolation. This text emphasizes the need for each member of a production to know well the work of every other member. At the same time, weight is placed on the need to acquire more than an intellectual understanding of the fundamentals of acting and directing. You will want to grasp the terminology and develop the skills so that they become tools that are instantly available to you. The format of this book is designed to encourage you to apply these tools to specific techniques in the production process.

The discussion of acting focuses on the expressive use of voice and body, stage orientation and usage, building and refining characterizations, performing, and hints for working with a director. The suggested techniques and exercises are designed to aid you in acquiring the essential performance skills.

The section on play directing describes the function and work of the director. It includes director responsibilities, the pre-rehearsal processes of analysis, consultation, and preparation of the prompt book, and procedures for rehearsals. (Play selection, try-outs, and casting, although responsibilities of the director, are omitted here because they do not necessarily call for collaborative skills.) Suggested techniques and exercises are provided for practical workshop purposes, as well as for discussion. The material is arranged so that those who find themselves thrust into a directing situation before completing an appropriate training program will have some helpful guidelines to follow.

Acting & Directing is intended to help you get started. As a director, you must be ready to supply the answer to the actor's "why?" As an actor, you must realize that sometimes the director simply does not have an answer. You do not need to be a good director to be a good actor — or a good actor to be a good director. But if you are aware of the roles of both actor and director, you will be more effective in any aspect of theatre collaboration.

— Russell J. Grandstaff

Part I: Acting

You probably are aware that the typical theatre-goer looks upon the work of the actor as "fun and games." You know, too, that some neophytes to the theatre, perhaps attracted by the apparent glamour, enter into acting and other theatre activities with the same "fun and games" attitude. Certainly, participants in theatre should enjoy their involvement, but they must realize at the outset that theatre in general, and acting specifically, are among the most exacting disciplines of any art form or profession.

To be a good actor you almost must have the stamina of a mountain climber, the endurance of a marathon runner, the patience of a turtle, the strength of a weight-lifter, the courage of a lion trainer, the memory of a computer, the agility of a gymnast, the imagination of a child, and the confidence of the devil. If you do not now possess all of these traits, don't panic! Remember that even the good actor had to begin sometime, somewhere. What follows are many of the things that good actors have discovered, practiced, and bequeathed to those of you who also aspire to be actors.

As a beginning actor you will need a point of departure to help you discover the nature and degree of your involvement. This segment of play production is designed to introduce you to the basic vocal and physical requirements of acting; the basic techniques; and a method of analyzing and developing characterization.

Application of the materials is no guarantee of success; your

1

own motivation to learn and apply yourself is more essential. Naturally, if you are properly motivated and possess abilities that are compatible with the art of acting, you will progress faster than those who have the inclination but lack the innate abilities. As consolation for the latter group (we are in the majority, by the way), there would be much less theatre activity in this country if it relied only on "natural-born actors." There is room and need for those who are motivated to learn.

Expressive Use of the Voice

It is disheartening when you realize or are made to realize that our normal, everyday vocal characteristics are the unfortunate products of a lifetime of bad habits and imitation of poor models. If you are sincerely motivated to improve your speech, it is even more distressing to learn that years of concentrated study and practice may be required to achieve significant changes. The beginning actor will find the rehearsal period of four to eight weeks too little time to develop a highly flexible and expressive voice, to learn and enforce proper breathing habits, to develop optimum pitch, and command and control the entire speech phenomenon.

Your director realizes that beginning actors possess varying degrees of vocal proficiencies. He or she recognizes the time needed to train actors properly for the stage, but will insist that you possess two vocal attributes, even if it is your first acting experience; you can be heard, and understood.

Being Heard

You probably have no difficulty being heard in normal conversational circumstances, and perhaps you will have no problem projecting your voice from the stage to the last row of the auditorium. If, however, your director indicates that you cannot be easily heard, or that you sound as though you are yelling, you may need to examine three critical factors of voice production: proper breathing, relaxed but controlled muscles, and opening your mouth.

Breathing

To check your breathing habits, stand in front of a mirror and say the entire alphabet aloud. Repeat the ABC's twice, breathing as you normally do. Then repeat the procedure, paying particular attention to the parts of your body that move noticeably when you inhale. If your shoulders and upper chest rise slightly, you are probably employing clavicular breathing. If your abdomen moves outward during inhalation, you are utilizing abdominal breathing. Of the two, clavicular breathing is more common but less desirable for effective voice production. Clavicular breathing creates a thinner, more shallow sound. It tends to cause one to constrict the muscles used in speech and it limits the degree to which one can control the breath stream.

People interested in improving their voice production should adopt abdominal breathing as a lifelong habit. As an aspiring actor, you will find it an absolute necessity. To accustom yourself to what abdominal breathing feels like, sounds like, and "looks" like, lie on your back on a firm bed or couch, or on the floor. Place your hands on your abdomen — near the rib cage — relax, and breathe. It is almost impossible for you to breathe improperly. Your hands should rise as you inhale and lower as you exhale. Now say aloud the ABC's, taking breaths after each group of eight or ten letters. Notice your hands rise when you inhale, but pay particular attention to the gradual lowering of your hands as you vocalize each sound. This demonstrates the manner in which your abdominal muscles control the stream of air needed to produce sound effectively. It is this control of the breath stream that you will want to gain.

After you experience the sensation of abdominal breathing in the prone position, stand up and again look in a mirror, placing yourself in a profile position. Repeat the alphabet exercise, inhaling after each eight- or ten-letter cluster. Are you able to maintain the same abdominal control that you possessed in the prone position? Your abdomen should expand with each inhalation, and you should feel the abdominal muscles contracting as you vocalize.

Do not interpret the process of abdominal breathing as requiring you to inhale unusually large quantities of air. It is not an endurance test to determine the length of time you can speak without stopping to inhale. Rather, take in as much air as your lung capacity can accommodate without causing discomfort or unusual bodily activity. Maintain control of the air stream by using the abdominal muscles.

Finally, practice economy of breath. You will find yourself with a large reserve of air if you prevent unnecessary leakage of air when you vocalize. To recognize the problem, whisper the ABC's. Go as far as you can before stopping to inhale. Now say them aloud. You should be able to surpass all of the whispered letters by a significant number, possibly even twice as many. Whispered speech demands more breath than vocalized speech. If your vocalized letters failed to exceed the total whispered letters, or only barely, you are wasting too much breath in your vocalized delivery. This means that you are probably permitting a constant flow of air to pass through the vocal bands. You must learn to conserve your air supply, controlling it with your abdominal muscles.

Read aloud the following series of letters, concentrating to see that no air is emitted during the intervals between vocalizations (take approximately eight seconds): A, B, C, D, E, F, G. Now read them aloud making certain that the air stream is sustained evenly as you proceed from one letter to the next (take approximately five seconds). Do you hear the difference? In the latter exercise you probably noticed a "hum" as you moved from one letter to the next. Read the following as though the clusters of letters were words in a sentence (be sure to shut off the air stream between clusters): ABC, D, EF, G. Substitute actual words and vocalize the sentence:

ABC	D	EF	G	H
I don't know	how	to do	that	But

IJKL	MN	OP.
if you'll show me	I'll try	to learn.

The point to appreciate is that you do not need to sustain the air stream between phrases or between sentences. Moreover, for effective voice production, for clear vocal quality, and for meaningful, image-making speech you should not permit a wasteful leakage of air. Once you secure and maintain abdominal control of the air stream, you will discover that the same set of muscles will help you project your voice to the last row.

Relaxation

A second critical factor of voice production is the relative tension of the muscles used in vocalization. If you have attended an exciting basketball game and participated in the event by cheering for your team, you may have experienced hoarseness. Chances are that if you could vocalize at all after the game the quality of your voice was rather unpleasant. One reason for this condition is that you subjected your vocal mechanism to excessive tension. Clear tones do not stem from tense throats. For that matter, tense muscles will hinder any performer: golfer, singer, piano player, or actor.

In your efforts to project your voice on the stage, without yelling, do not make the common error of contracting your throat muscles and raising your pitch. Within an hour, or less, you will be fatigued, hoarse, and ready to call it a day. (You could cause permanent damage to your vocal mechanism, too.) Instead, keep in mind what you have learned about proper breathing, utilizing the abdominal muscles to control the breath stream. Make certain your throat and neck are *actually* relaxed. This is the critical point, because too frequently people think they are relaxed when they are, in fact, as taut as a drawn bow string.

To realize the difference between relaxed and contracted muscles of the throat, try the following exercises. First, place an imaginary "horse" pill in your mouth and swallow it. As soon as you have swallowed the pill, say "dog." Did you notice the muscles of the throat contracting? Second, yawn as widely as possible, then say "dog." Could you hear the difference? Following the yawn, the utterance should have been clearer and more pleasing than that which followed the pill. Did you feel the difference? Your throat muscles should have been more relaxed after the yawn. Third, yawn again, breathe easily, yawn, and continue to breathe in and out two or three times. You should be experiencing the type of relaxed throat muscles that you need for effective voice production.

Opening Your Mouth

You may think the final suggestion for helping you to be heard is too obvious, too silly for consideration. *You must open your mouth!* Speaking through clenched teeth and firm, drawn lips while maintaining a concrete jaw is one of the most common faults of voice production. There is no better way to muffle sounds, to make listening difficult, and to fail to communicate.

In your consideration and practice of this concept, you will need to develop a vertical "flap" action of the chin, and a constantly enlarged oral cavity. The vertical action of the chin will help you to form appropriate lip positions to form your vowel sounds; and, will make it easier for you to resist stretching the corners of your mouth towards your ear lobes. The latter is a national disease — and a disgrace for an actor. The condition is referred to as a "lateral stretch" by some authorities. You'll recognize it if you will smile — a big, wide smile, with the corners of the mouth pulled back to the ears — then say, "I have a lateral stretch." Repeat several times and reflect on the sound itself, the flatness of the quality, the elongation of vowel sounds, the weak projection, and the lack of space for the tongue to maneuver.

For good sound and effective projection, and to provide adequate space for the tongue to function effectively, you must increase your awareness of the oral cavity. Is your tongue almost completely filling the cavity? What must you do to enlarge the cavity? You could let the chin sag slightly (keep your lips closed) and immediately provide more room for the tongue to rove about the cavity. If this technique works for you, go a step further and try to achieve the physical change by "thinking up" rather than dropping the chin. As you now read silently, slowly, and without strain, "think up." Gradually permit your head to drift upward toward the ceiling. (The exercise assumes a sitting or standing position.) Don't try to force the action. If you can make this work for you, you will receive at least four benefits: a larger oral cavity; a lightness, as though defying gravity; less tension in the neck area; and improved posture.

Learning to open your mouth presents you with a rather unique problem. It is really a matter of relearning what you probably did naturally as a child but have long since discarded in favor of a low-key, conversational quality. You will have to adjust to the "new" sound of your own open-mouth speech. The sound will be fuller, richer, and louder because your resonance will be improved, and the volume will be increased.

To appreciate the megaphonic potential of your own mouth, execute the following sequence of exercises. Clench your teeth, part your lips approximately one-eighth of an inch, and by maneuvering your tongue say aloud: "I tried that twenty times." Do not permit your lips to open more than one-eighth inch. (If you were unable to do it or if the words were largely indistinct, realize that not all people can grit their teeth and still speak.) Notice that your lips closed only one time—for the M in "times." Notice, too, that the nasal cavities carried most of the resonant quality.

Now do not let your teeth touch, and again do not part the lips more than one-eighth of an inch. Repeat the sentence: "I tried that twenty times." This vocalization should be clearer than the first, the quality should be more pleasant, and the volume a little louder. If necessary, to really hear the difference, try alternating the two exercises.

Now open your mouth until your lips are about one-half inch apart, making certain that the act is accompanied by a relatively loose jaw action. (The chin should sag a corresponding one-half inch when you part your lips.) Try to maintain this aperture for each of the vowel sounds: "*I* tri*ed* th*a*t tw*e*nty t*i*mes." Compare the sound when you speak in this manner with those of the first two exercises. You should be able to hear the differences distinctly.

At first, the very act of opening your mouth will seem unnatural, and you may imagine that your acquaintances are looking at you in a quizzical manner. There is nothing shameful and no reason to be self-conscious about being easily heard and readily understood.

Like all other facets of preparation, however, you must remember that the process of improvement begins now. Do not delude yourself by thinking you can start later. Start now to practice properly and constantly so that the entire speaking mechanism can be strengthened by production night. The training cycle is quite similar to the athlete's conditioning program. The football player does not wait until the week before the first game to build up his lungs and body. As an aspiring actor, you cannot put off your conditioning program until tomorrow.

Being Understood

To be understood means that your articulation and pronunciation are clear and that your pattern of phrasing words follows the "word cluster" manner of everyday conversation. You may need help to determine your own problems, because it is difficult, sometimes impossible, for people to hear their errors. Listening to a recording of your speaking voice may be helpful, but only if you possess the ability to discriminate between correct and incorrect speech sounds. You must develop a sensitive ear so that you actually hear the difference. Your director is well-trained to help you hear your mistakes.

Articulation
Articulation is the production of the speech sounds used to form words. Unfortunately, most of us develop slovenly articulation habits. We maintain a tight jaw, lazy lip and tongue action, and an improper adjustment of the vocal folds to control the air stream. It is no wonder that the most frequently used word by Americans is "Huh?" People simply cannot understand other people!

It is theatrical heresy for an actor to slur or slough sounds that need to be voiced in order to communicate. Are you committing some of the more common articulation faults? Do you sound the endings of words — endings such as *ing, ed, t, th, ness,* and *es?* Do you say *hello* or *huhlo?* Do you say *little* or *liddle?* Do you say *puddle* or *puttle?* In each of the last three examples, an inaccurate placement of the articulators causes the error.

Listen critically to yourself vocalizing the following series of words and phrases:

1. Putter, paddle, puddle, patter.

2. Tap the ball with the putter.

3. Don't step in the puddle.

4. Don't patter while putting.

5. He's paddling in the puddle.

Can you distinguish between the *dd* and the *tt* sounds? Notice the slightly different placement of the tongue on the hard palate when you vocalize them correctly. In 3 and 4, did you say *Don't* with a strong *t* or did you say something that sounded like *Dough?* In 3, did you provide *step* with a plosive *p?*

Read the following sentence aloud.

The bird began to build a nest in the fork of the tree, working hard to complete it before dark.

Were any of the sounds similar to those in this sentence?

The burr began to bill a ness in the for uh the tree, workin har ta comple it bfor dar.

Repeat the first sentence, slowly. Reflect on how easy it is to slough word endings. Notice, too, that it takes more effort to articulate correctly and to include every word ending when you vocalize.

If you claim that you are "sound perfect," that you hear yourself articulating every sound correctly, then you are in trouble, and you need help. (The odds that you articulate perfectly are heavily against you.) The problem is that you may be hearing what you want to hear, not what you should be hearing. To those who argue, "What difference does it make?" the answer is simple. If actors continue to commit common articulation errors there is a 99 percent chance that they will not be easily understood. If you are not understood, you fail to communicate with an audience.

With the help of your director, determine several sounds that you habitually articulate improperly. Then plan an improvement program that includes practice and careful monitoring. You may choose to select a list of words that includes your troublesome sounds or you may want to read from prepared materials. A long speech from one of Shakespeare's plays would be an excellent exercise. Many of Ogden Nash's poems demand superior articulation.

No matter what material you use, practice is only as effective as its monitoring system. The adage, "Practice makes perfect," should be qualified to read, "Correct practice procedures may tend to lead a person toward some degree of perfection." As soon as you learn to distinguish sounds — actually to hear what you vocalize — you can monitor yourself. Recognize, however, that when you practice in private you are not really putting yourself to the test; in private, you are concentrating on particular sounds. You will probably become quite proficient, but how do you articulate in your conversations with people? Here is the test, because in casual conversation we tend to relax. Our articulation becomes slovenly. If you can avoid this pitfall and if you strive to remain highly conscious of your improved program, you should make significant improvement.

Pronunciation

Pronunciation, the process of placing sounds in order, is a second basic factor in being understood. "Sgoeet" may serve to invite a buddy to have lunch with you and "Glatameecha" may tell a new acquaintance how you feel about being introduced, but either phrase, when spoken by an actor on the stage of a theatre, may fail to create the necessary mental image in the minds of the listeners.

You must learn to listen objectively to your own pronunciation habits and work diligently to improve them. One practical guideline is to listen critically to others and determine their errors. The point is not to call attention to the other person's mistakes; rather, you reflect on whether or not you're making the same mistakes. In other words, you use the vocalizations of others as a monitoring system for yourself.

If you have articulation problems, your director may ask you to speak in an overly precise manner during the early stages of rehearsal. Naturally, you will sound artificial — certainly an un-desirable quality — and you will feel self-conscious about it, but it is much easier to soften the edges of overly precise speech than to build gradually to the desired level of excellence.

Phrasing

In normal, everyday conversation we use a combination of simple sentences, fragments of sentences, and complex and compound sentences. (Many complete thoughts are expressed with grunts, whistles, and sighs.) Generally, we unconsciously break up sentences into short, meaningful clusters of words, inserting pauses of various duration between the clusters. To breathe life into dialogue you must follow the same practice.

If you said to a friend, "I finally got a date for the dance Saturday night," you probably vocalized the statement in three or perhaps four distinct phrases.

I finally got a date/for the dance/Saturday night.

I finally/got a date/for the dance/Saturday night.

Listed below are examples of common pronunciation errors:

Sound Omission and/or Substitution
recognize — recanize
realize — relize
surprise — saprize
yellow — yella
gesture — jester
endless — enless

Sound Addition
athlete — athelete
remnant — remanent
chimney — chimaney or chimaley
umbrella — umberella
wash — worsch
Illinois — Illinoise

Misplaced Accent
po*lice*man — *po* lice man
*the*atre — the *ate* er
*pro*gram — pro *gram* or *pro gram*
deliver — *dee* liver
be*lieve* — *bee* lieve
de*cide* — *dee* cide

Sound Inversions
predict — perdict
production — perduction
relevant — revelant
exercise — exrecise
improvise — impervise
cavalry — calvary

Vowel Substitutions
can — kin
for — fer
get — git
tired — tarred
just — jist or jest
feel — fill

Probably each break, though slight, received a different duration pause. If the same sentence were a line of dialogue in a play, it should be read with the same principle of conversational phrasing. Unfortunately, it will too often be read as one long word of thirteen syllables: "I-finally-got-a-date-for-the-dance-Saturday-night." Compare the two readings and you will see that the latter does not conjure up the meaningful thought picture that the phrased reading did.

In addition to articulation, pronunciation, and phrasing, there are other attributes of the voice that will help you be better understood. Qualities of pitch, pace, inflection, and stress also have significant influence on effective communication. They should, however, be studied under the tutelage of a trained voice and articulation teacher. If you are seriously motivated to improve your speech, concentrate first on developing proper breathing habits, and then improve the sounds that you project.

Expressive Use of the Body

If there is any truth to the statement that "acting is action," it argues that the actor's body is one of the principal means of expression. When we watch a competent, well-trained actor stand, sit, walk, and gesture on the stage we do not really reflect on the execution of these actions. We respond to the message the actions communicate. For example, an actor hears the telephone ring, rises, crosses two steps, hesitates, then slowly completes the cross to the telephone, hesitates again, and picks up the receiver. If properly executed, we do not analyze the actor's physical action; rather, we observe the character is hesitant, indecisive, perhaps even frightened at the prospect of answering the telephone.

Emotions, attitudes, and relationships are revealed through use of the body. Actors must have such control of their bodies that they can produce a desired physical action instantaneously, effortlessly, and convincingly. Frequently, an actor is directed to sit in what is an extremely awkward position and yet give the impression that he or she is quite comfortable. An actor's body must be conditioned to perform unusual as well as routine actions in an unlabored, believable manner. Anything less will call attention to itself and detract from what is important.

As an actor, the manner in which you stand, move, and

gesture are the impressions that an audience receives. Unless the script demands the contrary, you never deliberately try to keep the audience guessing who you are, what you are, or what your thoughts and feelings are. The strongest impact is made on an audience when it "sees" the idea. Merely "hearing" an idea makes too little an impression — too insignificant an impact — on an audience.

Your job is to choose the physical characteristics that best define your role and distinguish it from all the other characters in the play. You select and develop those actions and postures that reveal your character's age, background, emotional structure, motivations, and relationship to the play and to the other characters. Then you shape them so that they are consistent and believable.

If your character is supposed to walk with a limp, you must ascertain which foot you will favor, and favor it constantly. Should you carelessly favor the other foot, or forget to limp altogether, you will certainly receive a hearty laugh from the audience, ruin the scene, cause your co-actors to lose their poise and concentration, and destroy the audience's ability to believe in your character. The same is true if you're not consistent in playing old age. For example, people in their seventies do not move as quickly as you. Their postures differ as well. Once you establish the fastest, slowest, and normal pace of the old age-character, and after you establish his or her typical body attitude, you must maintain them faithfully.

Believability means that the actions seem appropriate to the character. Even if the actions are established as basic to the character and are used consistently, you must execute them in a convincing manner. Awareness, relaxation, and coordination are your principal guidelines for creating a state of believability.

Stage awareness is the realization that stage acting is "just a little bit bigger than life." On the proscenium stage, small actions — especially facial and hand gestures — must be magnified enough to be meaningful to the vast majority of the audience, yet not so large that they are overdone or burlesqued. You must maintain an awareness of your stage environment, your physical relationship to the other characters and to the audience. Drawing a line between the well done, the overdone, and the barely begun takes time and experience. Heed the suggestions of your director, who is in the best position to help you find the appropriate level.

Singers, dancers, athletes, and actors are coached to relax; effective and expressive action cannot evolve from tense muscles and a taut nervous system. You must learn to control tension to the point that it does not interfere with the effortless execution of action. (Good voice production also is relatively impossible if the muscles that govern its use are constricted.) A football player, tight with tension, may fumble the kickoff. A singer, tight with tension, may not hit the highest note clearly and effortlessly. An actor, tight with tension, may stumble over a piece of furniture, slip on a step, snag his or her coat on a doorknob — or, more disastrously, call attention to that awkward action rather than to the character. A stumble, a slip, or a snag can be covered, but the remainder of the performance may be spent trying to convince the audience of the believability of the character.

There is no place onstage for awkwardness unless it is a purposeful bit of staged business or a characteristic of a role. Awkwardness caused by poor coordination or insufficient control is a serious problem. In a crowd scene involving fifteen characters, the person of poor physical control will, unfortunately, draw undue attention to him or herself. It might be slovenly posture, clumsy movement, or half-drawn gestures, but it *will* distract the spectator. It may be funny, but it is not a joke, to hear stories about how the spear-carrier with no lines came onstage, stood there, and ruined the scene. It *happens*, much to the distress of directors.

How does one gain control of physical actions? How does one develop more expressive gestures? You may already possess admirable powers of coordination and positive traits of carriage and movement. Your principal objective will be to refine them and adjust them for stage use.

Creative Movement

There are several things you can do to help make movement more appropriate and believable. Among these are many applications we label as *creative movement*. One approach is to simply observe then imitate the movement of others. Another is to allow the body to relax and respond naturally to various rhythms and moods of music. Isolating the movement of different body parts or suddenly changing the direction of your movement are exercises that will allow you to more effectively portray your character's movements. Additionally, badminton, dancing, fencing, gymnastics, and tennis are particularly useful activities that will help you develop balance and poise and improve your coordination.

Pantomime

Once you have practiced and begun to perfect some of the basic elements of creative movement, you are ready to apply your expertise to the art of pantomime. In addition to body movement, you must use your mind to relate to imagined objects, people, animals, or a variety of these to communicate a message or story without the use of words. If you are performing a story through mime, it is critical to keep in mind the elements who, what, where, when, and why. In addition, your audience must be aware of an obvious beginning, conflict, resolution, and conclusion to your story or you may be performing in vain. As with a performance on stage, your gestures, facial expressions, and actions need some exaggeration for the audience to successfully understand what you are communicating. Since you are relying on actions only, it is doubly critical to be the character you want your audience to perceive by assuming that character's posture, style of walking, use of head and body, and facial expressions.

Acting Concepts and Skills

Improvisation

An extremely valuable area of study for any young actor is improvisation, acting with little or no preparation. Although initial practice with improvisation may be done alone, the real test of your ability in this area is working with one or more other actors to improvise a scene. Just as with development of a role in a scripted play, you must keep in mind your primary goal as you develop your character and improvised scene: to determine and communicate a clearly defined intention through presentation of a logical sequence of events and actions. Normally you will begin with basic character information and with the circumstances in which you must find your intention (who, what, when, where, and why). Working with another individual or a group further complicates your task, since you do not know what they are going to say or do. You must respond in character and maintain believability as you adjust each moment to an ever-changing situation.

Remember to include a beginning, conflict, resolution, and conclusion in any scene you present. Improvisation is a good exercise for heightening perception, improving listening, developing concentration, and experimenting with variables of voice and movement for the actor preparing for a particular role. It also may be an end in itself. Numerous theatres and stage acts rely upon improvised scenes for all or a portion of their performances.

Dramatic Structure

An actor who wants to portray his or her character most effectively needs a clear understanding of: 1) the period in which the play was written, 2) the type of play, and 3) the style of the play or production. The first of these, the period, is normally broken into eight areas: Greek, Roman, Medieval, Renaissance, Elizabethan, Restoration, Nineteenth Century, and Twentieth Century. The Oriental theatre is treated separately. The type of play falls into five common categories: tragedy, serious drama, comedy, farce, and melodrama. Finally, the basic style of the play may be identified as either non-realistic or realistic.

Types and Styles

A brief look at each type of play will provide a little better understanding of their differences. *Tragedy* looks at life seriously as well as with something of a mood of exalted fascination. In a tragedy, the stakes are great, at least as the characters view them. We commonly use the term *universality* to refer to an all-encompassing situation or problem relative to human behavior as found in the tragedy. *Serious drama* differs from tragedy in that, while it may deal with a serious subject, it does not involve a catastrophic ending for the primary character or characters. In fact, the overall outcome may even be hopeful. While many believe that *comedy* evokes laughter, it may only cause a feeling of contentment or encourage a smile. Comedy gives audiences the opportunity to be detached observers, rather than to become emotionally involved as they would in either of the two previous types of plays. *Farce* is sometimes regarded simply as a type of comedy. It is certainly a more obvious way to elicit laughter for its own sake. Farce often uses gross exaggeration to accomplish its goal. The final type of play, *melodrama*, is usually sensational and romantic in its plot; and like farce, it uses exaggeration. Although a melodrama may have an overabundance of physical action, that alone does not make a play a melodrama.

To distinguish between non-realistic and realistic styles of plays, we might simply state that the latter presents the content of the play in a manner and sequence that gives the feel of real life, while the former does not have to create that feeling for us.

Elements

What exactly is a play? To answer this, you might simply list the possible elements of a play—elements that you are probably familiar with from a study of literature in English and reading classes. The first element is the organization of a play: *introduction*, which provides necessary expository information; *body*, which establishes some kind of inciting incident involving the protagonist in conflict with an antagonist and leading to the climax, at which time the conflict is resolved; and *conclusion*, which provides a summary. Other elements include the *plot*, composed of the setting and sequence of events; the *characters* involved; the *dialogue* they use; and the *theme* of the play. Additionally, there may be music or some spectacle that will enhance the overall effect. Another element for the actor to consider is the *subtext* or imaginary background which he or she may be required to visualize.

Stage Orientation

The language of the stage is codified, thereby simplifying the communication process between director and actor. Learning the nomenclature and terminology of the stage is relatively easy, after which you can respond quickly and accurately to direction. Orient yourself by imagining yourself standing center stage (*C*) facing the audience. Stage right (*R*) is always to *your* right. The stage direction, "cross down stage," means that you should move toward the audience. Down (*D*) is toward the audience; up (*U*) is away from the audience.

When a relatively bare stage is used, the stage areas serve as immediate reference points for stage movement. If furniture and recognizable units such as doors, windows, and fireplaces are placed in the walls of the setting, they serve as immediate points of orientation, but the code is still indispensable for communication purposes. In the floor plan below (Fig. 1), *A* is standing right (*R*) of the sofa (although the sofa is placed on left stage, the character is still on the right stage side of it). *B* is down left (*DL*) of the sofa. On right stage, *C* is down right (*DR*) and *D* is up left (*UL*) of the table. *E* is the down-right (*DR*) stage area. Since there is no set or floor property piece to which to relate *E*, we must allude to the specific stage area.

The full front position is such a strong position that it is reserved for special occasions. The beginning actor should use it only when it is specifically called for by the script, or when the director authorizes it. Most acting is contained within the one-quarter and three-quarter positions. At least 75 percent of your time onstage will find you working between them (see Fig. 2).

Despite the myth that an actor never turns his or her back to the audience, the full back position can at times be employed to advantage. Your director may require you to use it. If so, resist the tendency to try to "cheat" with your shoulders and head so that some of your face can be seen by the audience. Such contortion looks awkward, and it certainly will not benefit the scene.

Note that the terms "open" and "closed" accompany the full front and full back definitions. "Open" means to turn slightly so that more of your face and body are visible to the audience.

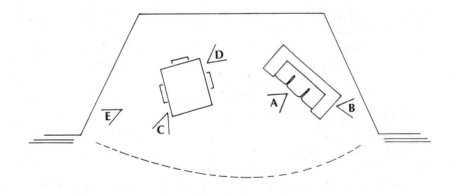

Fig. 1. Stage areas as reference points.

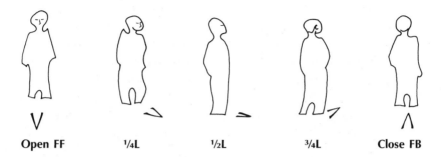

Fig. 2. Acting positions.

"Close" means to turn slightly so that less face and front of the body can be seen by the audience. For example, if you are positioned one-quarter left (1/4L) and your director tells you to open slightly, turn only a few degrees toward the audience, but do not turn completely full front.

"Sharing stage" is a basic position, one that must be carefully assumed and maintained. When two actors share stage, their positions are of equal strength. The principal sharing position places the actors facing each other in approximately one-quarter positions, equally open to the audience, their feet placed on the same board of the stage floor.

When standing, the weight should be distributed relatively evenly on both feet, but there should be no awareness of actual weight bearing. The cliché "light on the feet" should apply to every actor. You should be physically alert, able to move instantaneously and gracefully. If your role calls for you to contort your body, always retain a high suspension of weight and keep the torso aligned with the neck so that you do not impede the breathing and speaking mechanisms.

Sitting positions on the stage are seldom as comfortable as they are in the living room at home. The actor sits with regard for the fact that it is essential to be able to vocalize effectively, and that eventually there will be a need to rise. These two factors require that you never really settle back as though you were going to read a book. If you are directed to slouch, give the *impression* of slouching but keep your body alert, ready to move on cue and able to fulfill its function in support of your voice production. A key to sitting is to keep your torso in its standing position, with the spine aligned and head erect. Also, your feet and legs should be positioned in a manner to serve as levers and springs when you rise. Some directors insist that an actor, when seated, should support the entire body weight with the lower leg muscles. If the chair were to be removed, the actor should be able to remain in the seated position without falling backward. This may be stretching a point, but the principle is sound. Use the hips to support your torso and use the chair to support your hips. Try to avoid "lumping your weight" onto chairs.

Kneeling should be performed with the downstage knee touching the floor. This helps you maintain a slightly open position.

Relate to your audience. When you are standing or sitting, advance your upstage foot slightly so that a portion of your face is open to the audience.

Dress Stage

Automatically adjust your position to compensate for the movement of another actor. For example, if the focal point (action and/ or speaking actor) moves from one point to another, you should pivot or reposition yourself to maintain focus on the action. Dressing stage also means that you observe the rules of good grouping. This is especially important when three or more characters are onstage. Avoid a bodily attitude that is similar to the other characters'. Avoid standing in a straight line with two or more characters. Avoid grouping yourself so that equal spaces separate you from any two or more characters. Arrange yourself so that you are not masking (standing downstage of) another actor or an important object.

Do not "look for pennies" on the stage floor. Self-conscious performers tend to look at the stage floor, but the trait should be broken as quickly and permanently as possible. Garbled tones usually are emitted from this stance, and certainly the audience needs to see more than the top of an actor's head.

Movement

All movement must be motivated, and you should ask yourself the following questions. Why move? What direction? How fast?

What sense of force or energy should be apparent? How should it be related to the line? What physical and emotional qualities should be characterized by the move?

Almost all movement, gesturing, and business is carried out on your own lines. Learn to hold your position and attitude. Refrain from shifting your weight, moving your feet, fidgeting, or committing any other distracting activity when it is essential that audience attention should be on another actor. The only exceptions include your director's suggestions, specific demands of the script, the probability that you will have to adjust your position if the speaking actor moves, and the obvious need for a physical response to what is said. In each case make your adjustment as unobtrusive as possible.

Walk lightly and effortlessly. If the focal point of your body weight is carried high rather than on the feet, you should be able to glide across the stage gracefully and effortlessly. Strive to keep the shoulders squared, neither tilting them nor swinging them. Your head and shoulders should maintain a constant distance from the floor during a cross. Avoid bouncing up and down. Permit the knees and hips the freedom to fulfill their natural functions and allow your arms to swing gently so that the torso does not appear to be stiff. Lead with the nearest foot. When you move, step off with the foot nearest your destination.

Use a combination of straight line and shallow curve crosses when you move about the stage. The shortest route is usually your best traffic lane. The straight line should be your first choice, using the shallow curve when furniture or other actors stand between your starting and terminal points.

Crosses are made downstage (below) of standing characters and upstage (above) of seated characters. If your cross is dramatically important, avoid crossing above bulky pieces of furniture. A sofa, for example, masks the lower portion of your body. It may reduce the impact of your cross under certain circumstances.

The counter-cross, or counter movement, is a compensating action that is used to rearrange the stage composition. You should learn to effect it effortlessly and without calling attention to the movement. If you are sharing a scene and the speaking actor crosses below you, stops, turns, and continues the line, you should follow the movement by turning and continuing to focus upon that actor. Occasionally you will have to move up or down stage a step or two if the shared position is to be maintained. When three actors are onstage, the actor who is crossed may move into the area vacated and continue to focus on the action.

To *give* stage and to *take* stage are adjustment movements for the purpose of establishing a more dominant or less dominant position. Generally, both originate from the sharing position at a moment when the speaking actor needs stronger focus. To give stage the non-speaking actor closes position slightly while moving downstage a foot or two and continues to focus on the speaking actor. The speaking actor opens position a few degrees. To take stage the speaking actor moves upstage, while the non-speaking actor merely closes position slightly.

Backing up, or walking backwards, is by far the weakest move an actor can make, and this should be used only when it serves a required dramatic value. Too frequently it is employed by actors who attempt to clear the traffic lane for another actor's cross. If clearance is needed, turn slightly and step upstage; then reposition yourself.

Ascend and descend steps lightly and effortlessly. Each step you take should raise or lower your head a corresponding number of inches. If you ascend a three-step unit, each riser being six inches, you should be exactly six inches higher with each step you take. Again, avoid the bouncy movement, which, when you are on the ball of your foot, would increase your height another inch or two. Most directors insist that actors learn to maneuver on steps without looking at them. This demands that you carefully plot and practice all step movements well in advance.

Entrances and Exits

Begin your entrance well offstage. This means that you must be in character several moments before you enter and that you are fully in character as you carry yourself onstage. (Have you ever seen an actor, playing an old, old man, suddenly assume the old man's position just as he enters? Fine way to blow a scene!)

Carry your entrance well onstage. Ordinarily, entering characters have lines to speak. If there is a door in the door unit, you will have the business of opening and closing the door, speaking your line, and crossing onstage. Your guideline is to segment the speech so that it covers the door business and the cross. (*She enters, sees the guest.* "Hello." *Closes door, crosses as she speaks.*

"I didn't know you were here.") Your director determines those entrances when you linger in the doorway for a few moments, framed by the opening itself.

When two actors enter together, the speaking actor enters last. If three actors make a simultaneous entrance, the speaking actor should enter second or last. This allows the speaker to keep a relatively open position while addressing those who precede.

Break up the exit. Usually you will have an exit line. Learn to cover the cross and exit with the line, making certain that the last few words, at least, are spoken near the exit itself. This may require segmenting the speech. ("O.K." *Picks up hat.* "You'll never see me again." *Hand on doorknob.* "I mean it." *Opens door.* "Good-bye." *Exits, closing door behind.*) Carry your character completely offstage into the far reaches of the wings. When several characters exit together, the speaking actor usually exits last, or nearly so. In most instances that character is not the first to leave.

Turns

Most turns are open, toward the audience; but often the closed turn is more motivated. Let your director determine those instances when the closed turn should be used.

Use a sequence of action. If you turn to make a cross, to pivot in order to focus on a different character, or to react to another character, employ a natural sequence. Begin with the eyes, then the head, then the torso, followed by the legs and feet. A common error is to attempt to maintain foot position and awkwardly turn the torso and head.

Gestures

Follow through with gestures. A baseball pitcher follows through with every pitch. When the pitcher misses the plate too frequently, one of the first things the coach checks is the motion after the ball leaves the pitcher's fingers. A gesture that is only half performed or weakly executed lacks clarity and purpose. Also, it may fail to attract the attention of the audience. Remember that on the proscenium stage gestures have to be a little bit bigger than life.

Avoid using gestures that temporarily mask your face or the face of another actor. Usually, large gestures are made with the upstage hand and arm. Similarly, the handling of properties, such as a telephone, is performed with the upstage hand.

Be selective. Actors practice an economy of actions. Select the most meaningful and characteristic movement, gesture, or business and discard all others. Work for a singleness of purpose.

Reaction

Acting is action and reaction. We have discussed the former, but reaction means that you continue acting when you are not moving or speaking. It means that you remain "in the scene" as long as you are onstage. One of the major differences between a "good" and a "not so good" actor is the ability of the former to remain in character, to react and respond to the actions and lines of the other characters. It is particularly difficult for some actors to sustain their characterizations through the listening portions of dialogue. You probably have seen some who seem to quit acting after delivering their own lines and look blankly at the floor, wall, or other character while the latter speaks then come to life again when their turn to speak arrives.

Do not anticipate. Avoid looking at the telephone before it rings, looking at the door before you hear a knock, reacting to a key statement before it has been uttered. When you make an entrance, look to see where the onstage character is located before speaking or crossing to that person. Sometimes actors forget, especially after weeks of rehearsal, that an "illusion of the first time" must be created for every rehearsal and performance. In other words, when you enter, you do not know exactly where the other actor is positioned; therefore, you look to see.

Do not make direct eye contact with the audience. If the style of production is such that you should look at the audience, wait for your director's indication of where, when, and how. Direct eye contact destroys the dramatic illusion for the spectator and is a good indication that the actor is not in character or "keeping the scene onstage." (The young actor who comes offstage having spotted a friend, relatives, and established the house count at 762 should go into the accounting business, not acting.) When you are positioned so that you have to look toward the audience, select a point on the wall, above the heads of the spectators, on which to focus your eyes.

Pick up cues promptly. Cues are picked up several ways: by speaking a line, by action, by both speech and action, or by a *meaningful* pause. Generally you should use the pause with economy and place primary importance on speech and action. Regardless of the method, cue pick-up must be thought of as providing the punctuation for the previous speech. You must be alert and ready for the final word of the speaker. Otherwise, meaningless pauses begin to separate the speeches. Static, dull, slow-paced scenes are the inevitable consequence. A tendency to pick up cues too rapidly can destroy dramatic effectiveness. Thoughts are given too little time to be assimilated by the audience. If your director tells you to pick up the cues faster, it means that too much time elapses between the cue word and the cue pick-up. As you work toward faster cue pick-up, avoid the tendency to read the entire line faster. The results of race-horse delivery can be as disastrous as plug-horse pick-up.

There are many more techniques that every actor should know, develop, and perfect, but those listed in this section are basic to the beginning actor. Remember, they are starting points for your initial experiences on the stage. Consider them as your general rules until modifications are clearly indicated by the script, the circumstances, or the director. A realistic goal for you should be to gain mastery of basic techniques so you can perform them routinely. Learn the stage terminology used in this section so well that you can use it and respond to it instantaneously.

Character Analysis and Interpretation

The discussion up to this point has centered on getting you started, stressing the voice, the body, and basic techniques to help you through your initial acting experiences. Unfortunately, time probably will not permit you to master the basics before you have to begin a rather specific program of study and development — building a character.

There are many approaches that may be used to create a characterization. The following is designed as a guide to assist you to develop the first few roles that you enact. After that, you may be inclined to devise your own best method. If we can judge from the accounts of a great many professional actors, no two actors approach a role in the same way.

Regardless of the approach, all good actors, professional and non-professional, seek a common goal — a characterization that audiences will find believable. To achieve the main objective, actors strive for truthfulness, not only in the actions and speeches of their characters but in their interpretations of the playwright's intentions. They work for a balanced production, one in which the ensemble is featured rather than an individual. They labor to portray clearly the emotional, intellectual, and physical contents of their characters. Hopefully, these represent your objectives.

To begin, you must read the entire play, several times. Your first reading should be, ideally, in a single uninterrupted sitting, trying not to concentrate on any specific facet of the play or your own role. Read for enjoyment, for the overall impression. The second reading should be for thorough understanding of the entire play, still without concentrating on your own role. Read for clarification of the structure, the moods, the language, the ideas. Then read to examine the characters more closely, establishing their relationships, their distinguishing characteristics, their functions in the play. During this reading try to determine why your character is in the play. What is his or her function, his or her contribution? You cannot proceed to analyze and study your own role effectively and efficiently until you understand the total script. Any attempt to bypass the first step will inevitably result in an inaccurate appraisal of your own role and in a great loss of time and effort.

The fourth and subsequent readings are for intense study of your role. For this phase you should make written notes of all the clues your investigation reveals. Later they can be sifted and categorized into meaningful evidence. What you are looking for, first of all, is every conceivable allusion to your role. This information is revealed through descriptions in stage directions (usually in italics or enclosed in brackets), through the speeches of your character, and through the speeches of other characters. Be certain not to overlook significant allusions to your character in those scenes in which you do not appear.

Physical Attributes

The information should be arranged in workable orders. The first order contains the *physical attributes* of your character: age, size, pigmentation, state of health, disabilities, unusual characteristics of walk, vocal characteristics, and changes (if any) that occur during the passage of time the play covers. Perhaps a single bit of information will apply only to a specific moment in the play, negating the possibility that it is a normal trait that you should incorporate into your characterization. For example, if a stage direction indicates that your character squints while reading a letter, and it is the only such reference in the script, squint when you read the letter but be cautious about using a squint as a major piece of personal business. However, if you find several allusions — *"squints," "having difficulty focusing," "peers over glasses"* — you can readily justify making the condition a major physical characteristic.

Environment

A second order of arrangement is *environmental*. What is your character's economic, family, religious, and social relationship? How does the character make a living? What are the conditions of work, play, dreams? In this analysis carefully examine the playwright's description of the setting. Often it will reveal environmental factors that are significant to your character's behavior.

Perhaps you will not need answers to all these questions; perhaps not all these questions will be answered in the script. However, screen the script carefully. Most good playwrights provide all essential information in their plays; they seldom underline it, however. You may have to decide upon an appropriate age or physical characteristic if the script fails to provide the clues. You may have to imagine the background or the trade or profession. Be sure to exhaust the script beforehand.

Intellectual and Emotional Make-up

With insights into the physical attributes and environment of your character, you are ready to make even more revealing discoveries — *the intellectual and emotional* make-up. Some of the following questions may guide you in this vital phase of your analysis. What are the character's thoughts, attitudes, dreams, aspirations, prejudices, preferences? What is the intellectual level? Emotional stability? How does the character react under certain circumstances? Respond to other characters? Is there some sort of pattern or habit of behavior?

Function and Motivation

Finally, you should determine your character's *function and motivation* in the play. To determine function, establish the reason your character is in the play and the purpose served. To determine motivation, look for the clues that tell you what your character *wants*. What is the want or motivation in the play? What forces in the play are in opposition to the character's real motivation? The answer to the last question reveals the conflict—probably the principal reason for your character's existence in the play.

Observation and Concentration

The work of the actor continues. Now you must translate the information into expressive action and meaningful line reading. Then you must refine and polish the total characterization readying it for performance.

During these phases you will need to call upon two vital powers: observation of self and others, and concentration. Let us fabricate a situation. Your character is a sixty-year-old man, in relatively good health, married, and no children living at home. You drive a bread truck. Your wife has cancer. You will retire in two years. The house is mortgaged. Midway into act one you enter the kitchen of your home to announce that you have been fired from your job.

If you have not habitually and consciously observed sixty-year-old men you have to launch a crash observation program. Do not pick out just one man to observe; his characteristics may be too atypical. Observe as many as time and circumstances permit. How do they walk, stand, turn? What is their normal walking pace? Analyze the muscle structure of their faces. How do they carry and use their arms and hands? How are their spine, mid-section, and shoulder attitudes different from your own? Are their facial, bodily, or vocal mannerisms applicable to your character? How do they sit, rise, lie down? How do they open and close a door? Pick up a coffee cup? Read a newspaper? Does a man who has driven a truck many years walk differently from other men?

In our fabrication, the man is suffering some degree of shock and disbelief, and probably he does not relish the idea of informing his wife that they will lose their home, that he will have difficulty finding another job, that his retirement income may not be forthcoming. Probably you have never experienced this man's plight, but you are creating this role and you want to play it with a sense of truth. Somehow you must understand the emotions. Start by assessing your own experiences.

Can you recall a moment in your life when the entire world seemed to cave in? Have you ever tried to withhold information out of consideration for the feelings of another person? Have you experienced sieges of depression from which there seemed to be no relief? Have you felt a lump of emotion in your throat that restricted your speech, that could not be swallowed, that you tried to conceal but couldn't? How did you feel, behave, and speak under these circumstances?

Some of these feelings, behaviors, and speech traits may be helpful, but, in transferring them, strive to use them as the character would experience them, not as you experienced them. This means that you must *imagine* how the sixty-year-old man would reveal these emotions.

Concentration refers to many facets of the actor's work. In the creation of a role its major function is in helping the actor attend to a specific situation. It demands a sensitivity to language, to what is happening, to the situation. It demands that you "remain in the scene," that you close out all distractions.

If at first you have difficulty acquiring high-level powers of concentration, begin by thinking about what you are saying, about what others say. Listen and "think the thought." Your speeches and responses will take on sensations of truth and believability. Remember, however, that no emotion, no matter how truthful, has merit until its impact is felt by an audience. Your basic techniques are essential to the effective expression of an emotion.

Polish and Performance

During the final phase of your work you will strive for refinement of all movement, business, and gestures; to perfect the timing of all lines and action; and to reinforce the justification for all that you do. You previously should have been thinking about how you will look — your make-up and costume. You also should have been working with simulated or actual properties and accessories. Dress rehearsal is too late to begin handling an important prop such as a gun, a hat, a sword, or a teacup and saucer. It is also too late to refine the business of handling a hoop skirt, a bulky overcoat, or an umbrella.

"Butterfly season" opens on the day of the performance. All healthy performers—actors, athletes, musicians, singers, speakers—experience some degree of stage fright. It is not something that you should want or even try to overcome—try to *control* it, using it as a device to keep you alert. The fear process is a healthy and normal body function by which increased amounts of energy are produced for the purpose of giving the performer increased chances for doing well. If one believes fear is bad, the belief itself tends to produce additional energy, and this additional energy is not useful. Blushing, increased perspiration, increased heartbeat, some trembling and a feeling of "butterflies" are normal activities that occur when the body produces that needed and desirable increased energy flow. Try to accept fear as a normal condition and distract yourself from anxieties by concentrating fully on preparing your entire system for the performance. Loosen up. Warm up. Examine your system for tensions. Recognize them. Control them. Get rid of them. If you focus your attention on these processes, you won't have time to think about the nervous self.

If you are motivated, you will develop even greater powers of concentration, and you will be better prepared for your next acting experience.

Working with the Director

Your director assumes responsibility for everything that happens on the stage in front of an audience. The role is somewhat like the football coach, who carefully prepares players for a game but cannot go on the field and play the game. There is no control over fumbles, missed tackles, or intercepted passes. The coach has one advantage over your director, though, in that a time-out can be called to make a substitution or to slow down the momentum of the opposition. Theatre convention dictates that your director cannot stop the proceedings. The director, however, is the final decision-maker on all matters of production.

You, then, must realize that not all that you create and develop will be appropriate to the production as a whole. Certain modifications will be necessary from time to time. Realize that you are only one of the many components of composition the director employs. You must be a flexible element, aware of the director's vantage point.

Your experience in the theatre should be pleasant even though, as an actor, you may be required to work harder, concentrate more intensely, and cooperate more selflessly than ever before in your life. Such involvement, such discipline, can be pleasant. Your most significant reward for your participation should be the development of a high sense of pride: the pride that one experiences for having taken part in a demanding, rigorous effort; the pride one receives from an act of creativity; the pride gained from participation in a worthwhile production of quality. The applause of the audience and the congratulations of friends are only brief reminders of your efforts — and, perhaps, inaccurate gauges of the merit of your efforts. Actors, like all other artists of the theatre, must have pride in their work. The level of pride that you develop will depend almost entirely upon the seriousness of purpose with which you invest your time, energy, intellect, and learning potential. "Break a leg!"

Suggested Activities

1. Prepare a voice, pronunciation, and articulation self-analysis. Have a competent person listen to you speak and read. Take the suggestions given and place them in a notebook. Prepare a set of exercises, taken from the chapter, and practice.

2. Secure the use of an 8mm movie camera, and use fast film (Perutz); or secure the use of a video-tape recorder. Memorize some lines and develop some movement to go with them. Have your acting recorded, then watch it critically.

3. Play the game of charades, using lines or titles from some of the plays you have read.

4. Prepare a physical-fitness routine for yourself and learn at least one new skill each semester; i.e., dancing, fencing, tennis, etc.

5. Have one of your classmates take the stage; give fast directions for moving him or her about the stage by using the terminology for stage space and movement.

6. With two or three classmates, take the stage and move about it, demonstrating your knowledge of taking, giving, and sharing stage.

7. With at least one other classmate, demonstrate your ability to perform crossing movements.

8. Select a brief scene from one of the plays you have studied; prepare to act out one of the characters in the scene. Present the scene for your classmates. Have them give a response and then re-do the scene, showing them what the critique did for you. You might have the teacher be the critic.

9. Discuss the question, "Is stage fright normal and desirable?"

10. View a movie or attend a play with your classmates. Discuss the acting skills and techniques observed.

11. Given an emotion, demonstrate to your classmates that emotion in such a way that they are able to determine what it is.

12. Working in pairs, determine a situation, setting, and characters for a tag improvisation. Begin to work together in front of the class. As soon as another of your classmates feels she or he can pick up the body position of one of your characters, that classmate should shout "Freeze!" and tag the person that she or he wishes to replace. Change both the characters and the setting, and continue the scene from the same body positions with the new partner.

Acting Bibliography

Benedetti, Robert L. *The Actor at Work*. 3rd ed. Englewood Cliffs: Prentice-Hall, 1981.

Cohen, Robert. *Acting One*. Palo Alto, Calif.: Mayfield Publishing Co., 1984.

Cole, Toby, and Chinoy, Helen K. (eds.). *Actors on Acting*. New York: Crown Publishers, 1949.

Delgado, Ramon. *Acting with Both Sides of Your Brain*. New York: Holt, Rinehart and Winston, 1986.

Felnagle, Richard H. *Beginning Acting*. Englewood Cliffs: Prentice-Hall, 1987.

Harrop, John, and Epstein, Sabin R. *Acting with Style*. Englewood Cliffs: Prentice-Hall, 1982.

Hobbs, Robert L. *Teach Yourself Transatlantic: Theatre Speech for Actors*. Palo Alto, Calif.: Mayfield Publishing Co., 1986.

Kenyon, John S., and Knott, Thomas A. *A Pronouncing Dictionary of American English*. Springfield, Mass.: G. & C. Merriam Co., 1953.

Kuritz, Paul. *Playing: An Introduction to Acting*. Englewood Cliffs: Prentice-Hall, 1982.

Lessac, Arthur. *Body Wisdom: The Use and Training of the Human Body*. New York: Drama Book Specialists, 1981.

Lessac, Arthur. *The Use and Training of the Human Voice*. New York: DBS Publications, 1967.

Lewis, Robert. *Advice to the Players*. New York: Harper & Row, 1980.

McGaw, Charles, and Clark, Larry D. *Acting Is Believing*. 5th ed. New York: CBS College Publishing, 1987.

Morris, Eric, and Hotchkis, Joan. *No Acting Please*. Los Angeles: Whitehouse/Spelling Publications, 1979.

Shurtleff, Michael. *Auditions*. New York: Walker and Co., 1978.

Snyder, Joan, and Drumsta, Michael. *The Dynamics of Acting*. 3rd ed. Lincolnwood, Ill: National Textbook Co., 1989.

Stanislavski, Constantin. *Creating a Role*. Tr. by Elizabeth Reynolds Hapgood. New York: Theatre Arts Books, 1961.

Part II: Play Directing

Directing a play is in many ways similar to coaching an athletic team, leading a choral group, or conducting an orchestra. Each activity demands the responsible leadership of a well-trained person. If you have participated in any one of these programs, you already appreciate the need for a single, controlling hand. Can you imagine an orchestra led by two conductors, each with a different point of view? Can you imagine a basketball team coached by two people of equal authority, one insisting upon a "fast break" offense and the other advocating "ball control"? Can you imagine either activity supervised by an individual untrained for the particular position?

Your play director is the coach and conductor of play production, the guiding force. It is important that all theatre participants, regardless of their specific interests, have a clear insight into the authority held and the work performed by the director. Few people ever have the opportunity to direct a play, but actors, technicians, and members of the business staff need an understanding of their relationship to the director in order to more fully realize their relationship to the production. This section is designed to acquaint you with the work of a play director, to reveal your relationship to that person, and to serve as a guide for those who may direct a play.

35

What Is a Director?

Directors in the modern theatre stand as the controlling force for unifying all facets of the production of a play. They are multi-functional, multi-talented individuals who assume the responsibility for maintaining theatre as a cultural medium in our society. They are interpreters, teachers, and creative artists. Their powers of perception into human behavior must be keen; their sense of obligation to the playwright and to the audience must be sincere. By virtue of their experience and training, they possess organizational skills and a sound knowledge of the craft of directing.

It has been stated that the effective play director should be a combination of architect, sociologist, draftsperson, sculptor, choreographer, plumber, painter, carpenter, electrician, stress engineer, historian, nurse, drill sergeant, psychiatrist, anthropologist, costumer, musician, dancer, and public relations person — and really ought to know a little about acting, playwriting, stagecraft, and scene design. The truth is that people who have this background might have the capacity to be good play directors — but only if they also possess an unerring sense of the dramatic, so that they can translate a manuscript into a meaningful theatrical experience. This requisite cannot be taught, and it is doubtful that it can be acquired. The degree to which it is realized varies among directors.

The Role of the Director

Regardless of the organizational structure of the producing group, professional or non-professional, the role of the director is to interpret the play, create its mode of production, and prepare it for performance. The degree to which a director is solely responsible varies among organizations. At one extreme, for example, a director in the commercial theatre may work closely with the playwright in matters of interpretation. The director may create the style of production with the assistance of other artists — costume, lighting, and scene designers. Because most professional actors are well trained, having attained a high level of proficiency, professional directors usually do not have to teach basic acting techniques.

The other extreme is represented by a school instructor who has been commissioned to direct a play. This person studies the script and performs whatever research is necessary or possible for interpreting the play. There is not the luxury of designers to help mold the style of the production, and corps of loyal actors look for guidance in the initial steps of developing characterization. In addition, this director plans the publicity, promotion, and box-office procedures; builds and paints the scenery; assembles the properties and costumes; sets the lights; and even applies the make-up. In short, the entire responsibility rests squarely on this person's shoulders.

It may seem at first glance that the school director is at a distinct disadvantage — doing it all! As we have indicated, however, the example is extreme, although there are a few hearty individuals who follow such a pattern, by choice or because of peculiar circumstances.

In most schools which present a full-scale dramatic production as at least a once-a-year event, play directors assume full responsibility for the fulfillment of each facet of production. If they value their sanity, however, and the possibility of reaching retirement age, they *do not* attempt to execute every detail by themselves. Rather, they organize crews, each responsible for a specific technical or business assignment. They retain the authority to pass judgment on all elements of production and may supervise some of the crews, but they must delegate some of the work.

Other faculty members who have an interest or background in theatre, and those whose backgrounds can be applied to production, often become collaborators. If a school does not have a second speech-theatre instructor with a scene design or technical theatre background, the art instructor may be willing to help the director plan the fine points of the set design and set decorations. His or her knowledge of color, form, texture, and painting techniques can be of tremendous help. This, moreover, is an excellent experience for art students who become involved in stage-scenery painting techniques.

The director may ask the industrial arts instructor to superintend scenery construction and provide advice about how to use stage facilities effectively. In such a collaboration, the industrial arts students will benefit from the experience of building and rigging stage scenery. Likewise, the home economics and business instructors may be helpful in supervising the myriad details of costuming and business management. You can see that the possibilities for student involvement are almost infinite.

In schools where a theatre program is geared to two, three, or four productions a year, the director will still retain the all-controlling hand, but it is safe to assume that the production organization will be arranged to provide trained personnel—students and teachers—who will supervise and fulfill the various crew and committee assignments. No matter what situation students and directors find themselves in, the director must receive assistance in order to concentrate on interpreting, creating, and rehearsing. Pride in one's work can be realized only if there is quality in the product. A harried, harassed director seldom turns out a quality production. Without quality, the student participants are deprived of a large portion of what should be a truly enlightening and rewarding experience.

Under normal and realistic circumstances, then, directors assume responsibility for coordinating all production elements and for creating the conditions under which the play will be performed. They reserve the power of final decision-making in all matters of production.

As is true in any other position of authority, however, directors are responsible to others. They are responsible to the collaborative teams that they head. They are in league with the playwright, the actors, the designers, and the audience. They can never minimize the importance of others to the production.

The director recognizes the playwright as the main creative force in the production. The director's job is to interpret as accurately as possible the playwright's ideas and to present them in the most effective manner that will be meaningful to the audience. Any departure from this objective would destroy the collaboration with the playwright. Directors who use a play as a toy to exploit their own whims seldom approximate the author's intent.

Your director's association with those of you who aspire to act takes the form of recognizing that you will make your own special contribution to the play. Even if you are untrained and inexperienced actors, your vigor, curiosity, and insight will bring to a role appropriate qualities that the director could not have perceived without you. Your director is highly dependent upon your willingness to learn, to observe, to concentrate, to imagine, to invent.

As you receive continuing opportunities to develop acting techniques and skills, you will contribute to the collaboration to an even greater degree.

Our references to the designers of costumes and scenery are expedient ways for considering their relationship to the cooperative effort. However, all too often the director does not have a trained costumer and scene designer as working colleagues. Work is done with the assistance of students, committees, or faculty members who serve as artists or supervisors of these key areas. When working with trained designers, the director utilizes their abilities to develop the total pictorial concept of the production. While studying a script, the director conjures up mental images; some are vivid, but more often they are hazy. After determining the purpose of the play, the author's intent, the emotional and intellectual meanings, and the style of production, the director begins a series of conferences with the designers. Their specialized training and talent will supply all the details (the total pictorial values) needed to tell the playwright's story.

Though it may seem strange, the director actually forms an alliance with the audience. A production is planned with the audience in mind because it is as much a participant in the presentation as are the actors. The director cannot ignore the audience's theatre-going experience, level of sophistication, or reasons for attending the performances. Its acquaintance with various theatre conventions, styles of acting, and types of dialogue can be significant factors in evaluating the success or failure of a production. This does not mean that certain plays should not be presented because they have peculiar language or demand an unusual acting style. It *does* mean that the director must take pains to prepare a production in a manner that will be interesting and meaningful to the audience for which it is intended. Most dramatic literature is written to be played before an audience, with the intent that the thoughts and ideas be communicated through the medium of play production. To forget that the audience is a vital part of the collaboration is to forget a major function of play production.

The Work of the Director

As one of the artists of the theatre, the director divides his or her work into two distinct segments: pre-rehearsal preparation and rehearsals. Often, as many hours will be devoted to pre-rehearsal planning as to actual rehearsal. Like most successful operations, much planning and organization precede the finished product.

The director begins by studying the script carefully in order to know the play well enough to devise a point of view and determine an approach. Then he or she must consult, plan, and organize as much as possible in advance, because after rehearsals begin there is little time to devote to anything else. With the storehouse of knowledge gained from pre-rehearsal study comes the confidence that fewer "surprises" and problems will be forthcoming in rehearsals. Even if these were not valid reasons for advance planning, expediency would make the process worthwhile. For each hour spent in preparation, an equivalent hour is saved in rehearsal. Directors generally agree that too little time is available for rehearsals and that students' time-availability lessens yearly. Therefore, the efficient use of time is a critical issue.

The director who is unsure, unprepared, or poorly organized *may* come off with a good performance, but then again, he or she may be blocking act two on the night scheduled for the second dress rehearsal. To do justice to the play, the actors, and the audience, the director must "take the time that it takes" to perform the task. The time it takes depends on the director's background and training, and the nature of the play.

Pre-rehearsal: Analyses

If the play has been selected and the director has read it several times, the process of pre-rehearsal planning begins with an analysis of the script. The director will examine it for type, style, theme, structure, and the manner in which the playwright treats characters and dialogue.

Type

Determining the type of play is not ordinarily a problem, and an extra reading for this purpose probably is not necessary. The director, nevertheless, sets down in indelible fashion precisely what the play is — comedy, tragedy, melodrama, drama, or farce. Comedy may be subcategorized into "manners," "wit," "satire," or some other classification. If modern dramatic literature is being used, labels such as "gallows humor," "black comedy," "absurdist drama," or "serious farce" might apply. Regardless of the label that appears on the title page of the script, or the label that others use to identify the play, the director will use his or her own most meaningful term, one that can be communicated to the cast and to consultants. Many directors, weary of the numerous and often nebulous terms used to identify types of plays, prefer to place the literature into one of two categories: comedy and drama.

Style

Style is determined by the manner in which the play is written, by the stated intentions of the playwright, and sometimes by the director, if the script must be made meaningful to a modern audience. Many plays can be staged in several styles without hindering the playwright's purpose. Others, such as the bulk of classical dramatic literature, demand a particular style.

The simplest way to judge style is to relate the play to modern, everyday life. To what degree is it patterned on realistic human behavior? If it is reasonably similar and the playwright makes no attempt to imitate nature completely, the style falls into the general classification of realism. This means the director probably will plan a production that incorporates relatively realistic costumes, scenery, and properties with acting that follows the same style, creating the illusion that what takes place on stage is actually occurring. *The Diary of Anne Frank* and *The Miracle Worker* are plays that usually receive realistic treatment.

Plays that are written in blank verse, or with heavy patterns of rhythm and rhyme, or in any other fashion that departs from natural speech behaviors are non-realistic. The plays of Shakespeare and Molière are typical examples. Sometimes they are placed in realistic stage environments, but most frequently only suggestive scenic embellishment is used. Almost without exception, however, the style of acting that is necessary to properly complement a non-realistic play is a departure from reality, because demands of movement and language are unlike real-life behavior. No attempt is made to convince the audience that what it sees and hears is within the framework of everyday life.

In theatre organizations that have sufficient funds and equipment to provide suitable scenic backgrounds, directors subcategorize plays into various kinds of realism or non-realism; then they create a production whose total elements are consistent with that style. If producing groups are not as well endowed with funds and facilities (for example, black curtains have to serve as the environmental backing), it is sufficient that the director differentiate between realism and non-realism and concentrate on getting actors to fulfill the proper "ism." Few realistic plays absolutely demand a realistic setting. Few non-realistic plays play well in realistic settings. Each style demands its own acting style, and this is determined by answering the question, "To what degree is the play's language and action modeled on real life?"

Theme

The theme of a play is the playwright's statement, question, or view concerning human experience, human behavior, or the human condition. It is the unifying element for all that transpires in the play. It is the main thought under which subordinate, or supporting, thoughts and ideas are discussed or explored. The dominant theme is not always readily apparent. More often than not, good dramatic literature forces one to study carefully, to look beneath the surface, to determine the play's thematic statement.

A group of students was asked to discuss the dominant theme of Molière's *Tartuffe* soon after seeing a stage production of the play. The instructor was disturbed, but not surprised, by the variety of responses. One student thought the theme was the "funny" relationship between Tartuffe and Orgon. Another was convinced that "the dangers of a domineering mother" was the answer. "Be careful how you choose your friends" was popular with three students, and two students chose "greed breeds need." It was not until the class studied the play, the playwright, and the period in which the play was written that the concept of "religious hypocrisy" was unveiled and given serious consideration.

This example reveals the many ways in which a play can be viewed by people with various depths of insight or levels of sophistication. On the other hand, the director of the play may not have settled on a dominant theme. Thus, without a unifying central idea, the audience was free to make its own choice from the many possibilities that were pointed up in the production.

Little can be done to influence an audience's insight or sophistication. Some people attend movies and plays purely for entertainment, refusing to be lured into enlightenment or intellectual considerations. Yet, something can and should be done to correct the failure to understand the theme. The most expedient means is for the director to determine the dominant theme by a careful, critical study of the script, the playwright, and in some cases the period in which the play was written, and then to establish the theme's relationship to subordinate thoughts and ideas.

As in any other analysis, the director seeks information. How are the themes developed? Through what devices and characters? What is the playwright's statement or question? What is the relationship between the playwright's view and the potential audience? How will this view be received by the audience? To what degree will the cast be able to comprehend the significance of the theme? What difficulties will be encountered in trying to communicate the thoughts?

Plot

When analyzing the plot of a play, the director does not concentrate on relating the chronological sequence of events—what happens. Rather, the structure of the play is examined, and the placement of significant elements within the play are determined. Plays do not pour forth from a common mold; therefore, no single formula serves to analyze all plays. However, there are basic questions that can be asked. The answers will not only help to clarify the director's understanding of the structure but will tell a great deal about the relationship of the play's events. These data will prove valuable as the director plans the production and teaches the play in rehearsal.

How does the play begin? Are the initial pages of script devoted largely to exposition—the dialogue that presents background material? Does the playwright open with a scene of conflict? Typically a play opens with exposition sufficient to lead to an initial incident, an incident that sets in motion the action of the play. It is usually the point at which the audience begins to ask, "What's going to happen?" "Where will this lead?"

Does the initial occurrence, also called the "inciting incident," lead directly to the revelation of the major problem, issue, or question? Does the playwright employ a second and third incident and additional exposition before making the problem clear?

Most dramatic action and related events are built upon conflict between opposing forces. What are the forces? What are their respective motivations? Does the playwright arrange the sequence of incidents so that they eventually lead to a climactic moment, when the course of action favors one or the other force? What devices does the playwright use to sustain interest and curiosity? Does the introduction of unknown information turn the course of action, complicate the issues, or provide new insights into the problem? Does each incident stand more or less as a unit, with its own peak moment? Does one incident lead logically to the next?

Normally the chain of incidents leads to the major *climax* — that inevitable moment of confrontation between forces. Adjacent to the major climax is the *crisis* — the turning point that reveals the outcome of the conflict. Is the building to the major climax seemingly higher or more intense than the peaks reached in other incidents? Does the crisis precede or follow the major climax?

Following the climax and crisis, the playwright usually "ties a ribbon" around the package, resolving the unanswered questions still held by the audience. Is a logical outcome provided? Does the playwright answer the major question, or leave it suspended, challenging the audience to find its own answer?

Characterization

In order to analyze characterization, the director once again collects information and then assimilates it in a manner that reveals a character's motivations. Investigation into the dialogue and the stage directions is made, looking for allusions to each character. These data are categorized under physical, environmental, and psychological factors.

Physical and environmental factors generally are not difficult to determine. Playwrights usually reveal such basic facts as sex, age, and size in stage directions — or the action and the dialogue will reveal the essential information. The same applies to mannerisms, such as a particular type of walk or nervous habits. Environmental factors include the social and economic status of the character, type of work, religion, race, the physical conditions in which he or she lives or works, and the relationships and changes of relationships with other characters.

The discovery of psychological factors is more demanding. Here the director seeks insights into a character's emotional and intellectual behavior; how the character responds to various circumstances, affects the behavior of others, makes decisions, and the ethical values behind judgments. In short, the director must recognize what the character does and why. Analysis falls short of its goal if the character's motivations remain unexplained.

Generally, it is necessary to study the dialogue carefully to determine psychological factors — not only what a character says and does but what other characters say about that person and how they react to the character. It is not sufficient to note that a character "speaks sarcastically." The director must ask, "Why does this character speak sarcastically?"

Finally, the director analyzes a character's function in each scene and overall function in the entire play. What role does the character have in the conflict? How does this person contribute to the conflict? How does the character affect the outcome of the conflict?

Only through the laborious process of character analysis can the director properly prepare. Attempts to short-cut the procedure inevitably result in casting errors and inferior teaching in rehearsals. Although actors are told to analyze their characters in much the same manner, they need guidance from the person who has the total production concept in mind, whether on the school, college, or commercial level of presentation.

Dialogue

In the process of analyzing the theme, plot, and characterization, the director automatically becomes familiar with the dialogue, but it also must be examined for a few specific pieces of information. Does the dialogue seem to be activated, forward moving? Is there a predominance of short speeches or long speeches? Are long speeches of exposition, description, or introspection injected among short speeches? Having the answers to these questions, the director can prepare for certain problems in rehearsals. A series of short speeches will assume one tempo; a series of long speeches will assume another. A combination of short and long speeches demands a third tempo. Because of the elements of mood and atmosphere and their relationships to the dialogue, the possibilities for different tempos become almost infinite.

Long speeches sometimes are relatively static, especially in poor acting. Frequently, actors have difficulty trying to sustain the dramatic quality of a long speech. The director should look critically at the dialogue that builds to the climaxes. It is easiest to build peaks with short, briskly paced speeches. If the playwright uses lengthy ones, especially to build the major climax, the director may encounter difficulty in pacing the scene or in maintaining the measure of excitement that usually accompanies such moments.

Although sentence structure and the choice of words may seem insignificant, they, too, are critical elements in the analysis of dialogue. Long, complex sentences demand special skill from the actor and special attention from the director who works with the actor. Sense must be gleaned from each sentence. Breath control, relating the parts of speech, and attention to pause and inflection to establish meaning are a small portion of the interpretive process.

Words should be analyzed in terms of their relationship to the character and meaningfulness to the audience. If the play is by a good playwright, the director can only assume that the language is appropriate to the respective characters. The words assigned to a character are, or should be, consistent with his or her personality. Slang expressions, such as "cool," "neat," and "swell," are more the vocabulary of the teenager than the professional adult. Expressions such as "ain't," "he don't," and "had not never" are more the usage of a poorly educated person than a high school graduate.

Most of these considerations probably are studied carefully in analyzing characterization, but the director should not overlook the single-word or short-phrase speeches as they relate to the audience. This applies particularly to colloquialisms and uncommon slang, which might have different connotations throughout the country. In Shakespearean plays, many allusions to places, people, events, and things are unrecognizable to modern audiences. (Many modern allusions also are unrecognizable to modern audiences.) If words that appear in our modern dictionaries are used in play scripts but are non-communicative to an audience, the director must decide if they can be cut or changed without altering meaning or disturbing characterization. The fewer moments an audience spends pondering the meanings of words, the more moments it can devote to pondering the intellectual and emotional content of the performance.

Pre-rehearsal: Consultations

After the lengthy period of analysis, the director will have decided upon a point of view and determined an approach to the play. This prepares one for the second step in the process of pre-rehearsal planning, which is to consult with the designers or associates who will be responsible for carrying out technical matters. Decisions have to be made concerning the floor plan at this point, because the director must prepare a prompt book and the designer must prepare preliminary sketches of the setting. Most directors insist upon being actively involved in deciding the floor plan. Needless to say, they have the final word on what is finally adopted.

Floor Plan

Two major considerations guide the director in mapping out a floor plan: traffic patterns and acting areas. Both are related to the location of such set units as doors, windows, steps, and fireplaces, as well as to the placement of floor properties. A great many moments of grief can be avoided in rehearsal if care is taken in advance to provide ample alleys for movement and good areas for playing important scenes.

The director determines how many doorways or arches are needed and judges the relative importance of each. If a particular doorway serves as a major entrance for important characters, it must be placed to give maximum emphasis. Often it is placed in the upstage wall where characters will be suitably framed for focus and readily seen by the audience. A doorway leading to a kitchen, used only by a maid or for no more important action than to pass through to get a pot of coffee, may be placed in one of the side walls. Likewise, a closet door that is used only for storing garments may be placed in a side wall. But if some dramatic value is attached to storing garments, perhaps more significant placement of the closet door is necessary.

Other set units are treated similarly. A window that serves only a decorative function need fit only the logic of architecture — outside should be on the other side of the flat that holds the window. If, however, a character must stand beside and look through a window while describing an event taking place outside, care must be taken to place the unit properly. A side wall is the most frequent choice because it is easy for a character to open his or her body position to the audience while enacting the business of looking out and describing an action. The acting chore would be more difficult if the window were placed upstage.

Fireplaces generally are located in side walls. They are excellent units by which to place characters who are onstage, but who have no immediate function other than to focus on the action. Also, if a fire effect is needed, technicians will have fewer difficulties creating it, and the audience will not be distracted by the artificial flames. Often a fireplace that is used only for ornamentation is placed in an upstage wall, where it serves to break up the flat surface of the wall.

The placement of stair units is largely dependent upon the need to have the audience see them. In some plays, priority is given to the location of the stairway, even though it may be used only a few times. Molière's *Tartuffe* is such a play. The playwright expends two acts alluding to the title character before bringing him onstage, and the audience's curiosity is at a high level. It would be rather anti-climactic to have Tartuffe enter on stage level. Most directors of this play will insist on (and be willing to

Fig. 1. A well-planned acting and traffic arrangement.

compromise to get) an elaborate stairway, most likely with a landing attached, so they can point up this magnificent dramatic moment.

The arrangement of floor properties (furniture, mostly) is directly related to the placement of setting units. The director is concerned mainly that furniture placement provides suitable space for actors to carry on their dialogue, and that it will not impede the flow of traffic.

Normally, furniture of the living rooms of private homes lines the walls, with perhaps only a coffee table extending into the center portion of the room. An interior setting on the proscenium stage may use this arrangement to some degree, but certain modifications are made in order to relate the pictorial unit and the action to the audience. Onstage, some pieces of furniture follow the line of the wall, but important pieces, that constitute strong units around which actors will work and that afford good grouping possibilities, are placed farther onstage. The director knows that when blocking a play there is a need for a variety of movement to and from an acting area, variety in groupings within an acting area, and more than one strong acting area.

Again, the director determines what elements are essential to the successful production envisioned. Consideration is given to the largest number of people onstage at one time, how much traffic space they will need to avoid congestion, and the relationship of frequently used doorways to the placement of the furniture. Many directors will place onstage only those floor properties that are absolutely necessary. Their reasoning is that too much furniture may clutter the acting and traffic areas. On the other hand, too little furniture may give the stage a barren look and, more important, offer insufficient areas for the actors to group themselves comfortably. Directors are concerned, too, with the placement of bulky pieces of furniture, such as sofas. If they are positioned in a manner that masks the bottom half of actors using important doorways, they limit the theatrical value of entrances and exits.

In Fig. 1, notice that two major sitting areas are provided, that three strong acting areas are located downstage, and that three moderately strong areas are available above the furniture (shaded areas). Each area is carefully defined, yet the areas overlap slightly. Easy access as well as a variety of accesses to and from each area also is provided. Traffic lanes to and from the doorways are clear.

Characters entering through the main doorway, up right, would not be masked.

Compare this arrangement with the examples in Fig. 2. In A, furniture lines the walls. Most movement would be from left to right and from right to left because the major pieces to which the actors would ordinarily move are directly opposite each other. Crosses would be long and awkward. The huge, empty space in the center does not offer a single intimate acting area. Another drawback is the severe rake (angle) of the sitting units. Effective grouping would be difficult to achieve because the character seated downstage would be placed in an extremely weak position.

The arrangement in B affords only one traffic lane from above to below the furniture. The possibility of variety of movement is limited. Whether a scene is played above or below, notice almost all movement would have to follow the line of the furniture — from left to right and right to left.

In C, the grouping of floor properties is centered, a condition

Fig. 2. Limited acting and traffic patterns.

that invites a merry-go-round type of movement. Unless an actor squeezed between the upstage chair and the sofa, or hurdled the sofa (a movement seldom called for), it would be necessary to cross below the furniture in order to sit or to use the downstage acting area. Note, too, the steep rake of the sitting units.

As the director and designer agree upon a floor plan, the designer thinks also in terms of the actual setting. Knowing *how* the director intends to use the setting will be vital. Particularly, the designer will want to know to what extent actors will be running, jumping, leaning against scenery, slamming doors, and any other business that places unusual stress on scenic units. Stage technicians can accommodate reasonable amounts of abusive treatments, but they need the information in advance so that suitable reinforcements can be incorporated into the designs.

During subsequent sessions, the director should be in a position to make a definite and final statement of special needs. Considerate directors attempt as best they can to avoid "surprising" their associates at the eleventh hour with requests for special effects or unusual usages of scenery that is not built to withstand more than normal treatment.

Style of Production and Costumes
In this early phase of pre-rehearsal planning, the director also consults with the costumer, preferably with the scene designer in attendance, to discuss the style of the production and the use that costumes will receive. Although the director might not have completed a close study of the script, he or she should be able to pass on general concepts that the costumer can employ to complete research and begin initial designs. During this conference, too, the designer, costumer, and director need to explore the possibilities for color treatment. This is a mutual concern, an important matter. Neither one nor the other artist would want a chartreuse costume backed by a fuchsia setting, bathed in steel blue light (unless it were a particular scene in a revue). The vital issues are determining the general possibilities for color and reaching agreement that lines of communication remain open. Final decisions of such crucial matters cannot be made independently, and the director acts as the final judge.

Pre-rehearsal: Preparing the Prompt Book

The third and final stage of pre-rehearsal planning is the preparation of the prompt book. Only stage ghosts can reveal the number of play productions that have failed because directors "played it by ear." This is not to imply that it is impossible to present a good production with little or no planning, but it is a truism that few directors are capable of successful work this way. Those few are proven directors and usually have the luxury of working with skilled actors and other artists of the theatre for several hours a day over a period of several weeks. Most directors, however, have only a few precious moments of rehearsal, and, for the most part, are working with actors who are just beginning to learn the rudiments of acting. They do not have time to experiment as much as they might want, nor can they put the actors onstage and expect them to create their own movement and group themselves properly. Therefore, the process of pre-rehearsal planning includes the preparation of the prompt book. The director's consolation is that this tremendous expenditure of time will actually conserve time during rehearsals and make work more efficient. Consequently, the actors will have a more beneficial experience.

The prompt book is a point of departure. It already contains the director's reflections, jotted down during script analyses; notations related to style and possible approaches; and insights into interpretation and character relationships. Then the director visualizes the script in action, creating motivated movement, composing meaningful stage pictures, planning the control of audience attention. This process is called pre-blocking.

Pre-blocking

If pre-blocking had no other justification than establishing a point of departure and making rehearsals more efficient, it still would be valuable in that it forces the director into a close scrutiny of the script. The process pays off because it reveals many subtleties of the script that might not be realized until late in the rehearsal schedule, and perhaps not until the performance. It gives insights into the meanings of lines, the motivations of characters, and the relationships of characters. This intense study compels the director to know the play better than all the collaborators (except the playwright). This position of knowledge is essential to a position of authority as the guiding force for the production.

A good, serviceable prompt book should afford ample space in the margins for writing notes and stage directions. The ordinary play scripts that are provided by publishers may be sufficient for the actors, but the director needs more space for notations. A practical book can be made by disengaging a published script from its binding and mounting the pages on 8½" × 11" sheets of paper. ("Biology paper" provides a stiffer base and is more durable than ordinary stock.) A single copy of the script is sufficient if windows are cut in the mounting paper (see Fig. 3). A three-hole looseleaf binder provides a practical cover for the prompt script.

Stage Shorthand

Although the prompt book may be thought of as the personal property of the director, it must be an object of communication that others can understand. Most directors use a system of stage shorthand for entries. Inasmuch as the assistants to the director and the stage manager also may use the book, all entries should be clearly written and the usage of symbols should be consistent.

The following are relatively standard stage shorthand symbols:

X   = Cross, usually two or more steps

X5   = Cross, five steps

EnU = Enter, using upstage entrance

ExR = Exit right stage

EnL1 = Enter number one entrance, left stage (Entrances often are numbered, especially if there are more than one on the same side of stage.)

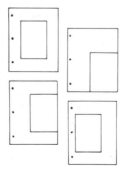

Fig. 3. Effective prompt book layouts.

When the stage is arranged with furniture, directors allude to the various pieces because they serve an immediate and convenient orientation:

XUL settee = Cross up left of settee

XDR table = Cross to down right of table

XU fire   = Cross to upstage end of fireplace

When the stage is void of furniture or set pieces, the director uses traditional segmentation of the stage floor as shown in Fig. 4:

XUL   = Cross up left

XDRC = Cross down right center

Various symbols are employed to signify "sit" or "rise," but a convenient set is the use of the arrow:

↓ chL table = Sit in chair left of table

↑ Xch2   = Rise, cross to chair number two

Some directors who use arrows to indicate other types of movement prefer to write out the complete words, "sit" and

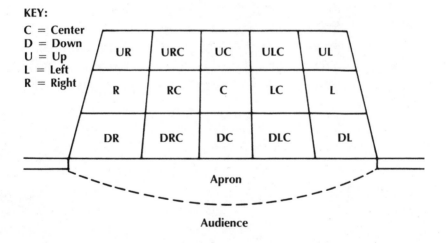

Fig. 4. Traditional segmentation of stage floor.

Open Turn   **Closed Turn**

Fig. 5. Indicating bodily movement.

"rise," and thus avoid confusion. Other uses for the arrow are for turns:

    = Open turn (front of body faces audience) from left to right (see Fig. 5)

    = Open turn, from right to left

    = Closed turn (front of body away from audience) from right to left (see Fig. 5)

Positioning also can be indicated by a symbol. A shaftless arrow is convenient, the point of the arrow indicating the nose of the actor. (The bottom of the page always represents the location of the audience.)

    ∨   or FF = Full front

    >   or ¼L = One-quarter left

    ⟋   or ½L = One-half left or profile left

    ∧   or ¾L = Three-quarter left

    ∧   or FB = Full back

The character's initial can be inserted in the arrowhead to indicate accurate relationships. A typical entry in the director's prompt book might look like this:

Fk. ⟶ XL table   F⟩   = Frank, closed turn, right to
left, cross to left of table, as-
sume a one-half left position.

This entry consumes much space and time if it is written out completely. (See Fig. 6 for a sample page of a director's prompt script.)

Some directors are able to visualize the floor plan and basic outline of the setting as they pre-block. Others find it necessary to have available a copy of the floor plan, which has been drawn to scale. Still others will make a model and include objects that serve as set units and floor properties. In using a floor plan or model, it is helpful to have the characters represented by suitable articles (toy soldiers, clothes pins, folded pieces of paper, or lengths of wire curled so they will stand). Directors frequently use such devices, pushing them around and maneuvering them in various combinations to create composition, movement, and control of attention.

In answer to the sideline wags who ask, "But why don't we use the blocking that's printed in the book?" most good directors prefer to rely on their own creative abilities. Besides, seldom will the stage directions provided in a published script be adaptable to the floor plan the director and the designer have devised.

Although directors may pre-block page by page, they keep in mind the total production and the possible staging of each scene. To maintain variety in the action and playing of significant scenes, they utilize the entire playing area when necessary, but concentrate most scenes in smaller acting areas. One highly emotional scene might take place around a kitchen table located right stage. The subsequent scene may be staged left stage near the rocker and fireplace area. The next scene may use center stage, where there are no floor properties. And a final scene of the act may utilize the entire stage. It is possible that this four-phase pattern might represent the staging of a single five- or six-page scene, especially if it is motivated by the action suggested in the script. The director decides where the scenes should be played—where they are most appropriately motivated—then stages characters into and out of those areas.

Usually a play is a series of pictures, some lasting merely a second, some as long as a minute. Each must be purposeful,

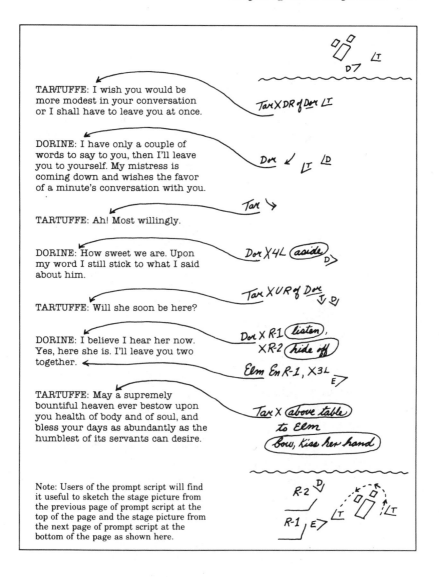

TARTUFFE: I wish you would be more modest in your conversation or I shall have to leave you at once.

Tar X DR of Dor LT

DORINE: I have only a couple of words to say to you, then I'll leave you to yourself. My mistress is coming down and wishes the favor of a minute's conversation with you.

Dor ↙ LT /D

TARTUFFE: Ah! Most willingly.

Tar ↘

DORINE: How sweet we are. Upon my word I still stick to what I said about him.

Dor X 4L (aside) D>

TARTUFFE: Will she soon be here?

Tar X UR of Dor ↓ D/

DORINE: I believe I hear her now. Yes, here she is. I'll leave you two together. ←

_Dor X R-1 (listen),
X R-2 (hide off)
Elm En R-1, X 3L E7_

TARTUFFE: May a supremely bountiful heaven ever bestow upon you health of body and of soul, and bless your days as abundantly as the humblest of its servants can desire.

_Tar X (above table)
to Elm
(Bow, Kiss her hand)_

Note: Users of the prompt script will find it useful to sketch the stage picture from the previous page of prompt script at the top of the page and the stage picture from the next page of prompt script at the bottom of the page as shown here.

Fig. 6. Sample of prompt script.

pleasing to the eye, help communicate the play, and establish focus on the most significant point. The director composes each picture carefully, dissolves it, and then creates another one. What the audience sees, usually without realizing it, is a continuous cycle of composition, transition, composition, transition. Without this action the stage picture and the production itself would be extremely static and uninteresting.

Movement

All stage movement should be motivated. It may be dictated by the dramatist as a significant part of the action; exits, entrances, a cross to a window to see something happening outside. It may be dictated by dialogue; "Come, sit beside me" or "Quit pacing the floor. You make me nervous." It may be dictated by the director for pictorial reasons, emphasis, or focus. Often the director notes how the move should be executed; for speed, emotional characteristics, forcefulness, timing, and final positioning. These considerations (as well as many others) also are basic to the work of the actor.

Aside from getting individual characters on and off stage and repositioning them while on the stage, several specific movements are visualized by the director. Their nature and the reasoning for them should be clearly understood by the actors because they will be expected to execute them. Two such movements are the cross *above* and the cross *below*. Crossing above means to cross upstage of furniture, people, or objects; to cross below is to cross downstage. Whenever possible and practical, the director wants an actor to cross below a standing actor and above a seated actor. There are times, however, when the desirable movements are impractical, and it is necessary to do the opposite.

Another specific movement that is used many times in every play is the counter movement. Imagine Character A and Character B engaged in dialogue, both standing. The director tells A to cross below B, and instructs B to counter, because A's speech not only covers the cross (almost all movement made by an actor is made on his or her own lines) but continues after the cross. The instruction to counter may be unnecessary for experienced actors. They know that the focus should still be on the speaking actor and will turn toward the actor who is crossing. A typical counter movement is illustrated in Fig. 7.

Fig. 7. Typical counter movement.

Composition

The pictures the director creates are called compositions. If the production takes place on the proscenium arch stage, each picture is evaluated in terms of its meaningfulness first and its artistic quality second. To be meaningful, a composition must serve the dramatic purpose of the scene. It should hold the emotional values and indicate accurately the relationship of the characters in the scene. Merely using actors to paint pretty stage pictures is not the function of the director. If the composition is faithful to the scene's motivation and is also esthetically pleasing, it is a bonus point for the production. Most directors learn quite early in their careers to be skeptical when they look at a stage and see a pretty picture. The first thing they ask themselves is, "Is the focus right and the composition meaningful?" If the answers are affirmative, the picture is acceptable.

Although the beautiful picture is considered secondary, each composition should render the artistic values that are found in most good painting. They should, for example, possess unity and balance, and each should also establish a focal point.

Unity is the quality of composition in which all elements of a picture appear to belong and to be related properly. All elements are in place; no single part distracts the viewer. To achieve unity the director strives to maintain a balanced stage and to control the attention of the audience.

A proscenium arch is to the stage picture what the picture frame is to the painting. Both provide a basis for analyzing balance. For this reason, imbalance is much more noticeable in proscenium staging than in arena or central staging. The problem for the director in pre-blocking is to visualize impressions, forcefulness, or the sheer capacity to attract the eye that each of the components will have onstage.

The scene designer will provide a setting that is balanced. When furniture is arranged, the stage picture still will be balanced. If an imaginary line were drawn dividing the entire left portion of the stage from the right portion, the two segments should give the illusion of being of equal weight, force, or significance. These forces, unless the scenery or furniture are changed, remain constant. The director then must measure the relative force of actors in the already balanced picture.

Symmetrical balance is the easiest form to achieve but generally is the least appealing. Except for a deliberate formal arrangement, for a musical number or comedy effect, symmetrical balance is generally avoided. Figure 8 shows two examples of symmetry. Forces on either side of the dividing line appear to be equal, because the size and shape of the objects are about the same, and the spaces between the line and the objects are similar. The pictures are not interesting; they lack motivation. Moreover, they do not command the eye to a common focal point, a factor that the director must seek.

Fig. 8. Symmetrical balance.

Asymmetrical balance is the servant of the stage director. With this tool, arrangements become more interesting, greater variety can be achieved, and a focal point can be established more readily. This kind of balance also can be examined by using an imaginary center line to divide the frame of the stage into left and right halves. Rather than trying to *make* the opposing forces equal, however, the director tries to *give the impression* they are equal. The regularity that identifies symmetrical balance is avoided by using a good sense of proportion. For example, in Fig. 9A, the objects on right stage are balanced by the single object on left stage. This illusion is created because of their relationships to the center line. (It must be remembered that the framed stage automatically creates an imaginary center line.) The left-stage object is placed farther from the center to neutralize the greater weight of the two right-stage objects. The same principle is seen in Fig. 9B, where the bulk of the right-stage object is equalized by the proportion of space and height of the narrower block.

Thus far, balance has been considered in terms of the total stage, with the frame and an imaginary center line as criteria for examination. From this it would seem that the director always blocks a two-character scene by placing one actor on each side of the center line, using a computer to determine the proportion of space, height, and girth. This, of course, is not true. If it were, all scenes would be played near center stage, and other acting areas would be used only for movement.

Actually, two or three characters seldom upset the balance

A   B

Fig. 9. Asymmetrical balance.

Fig. 10. Imbalance.

when they work in any of the acting areas of the stage. Their relationship to each other and to the floor properties creates a focal point that reduces the significance of balance. Directors are mainly concerned with imbalance when the script requires five or more characters onstage at the same time. Figure 10 illustrates the problem. The figure on left stage is insufficient to balance the picture. Imagine, however, the figure in a highly defiant physical attitude, hurling challenges at the mob to try to subdue them. Under these circumstances, the picture may appear to be balanced because the psychological or emotional force of the figure adds power to offset the physical size of the mob.

Focus
Each good stage composition has a dominant focal point, a central point of interest, which commands the attention of the audience. It may be a character, a group of characters, an open door, or an object located somewhere on the stage. Usually it is a character whose actions must be seen or whose lines must be heard in order to advance the scene. As one composition dissolves and another is formed, the focal point should continue to center on the most essential element in each successive scene, even though the most essential element may be different in each composition. The director must constantly calculate the relative importance of

each component in each composition, striving to focus audience attention on a particular point of interest. Restated, it is accurate to say that the director is actually involved in directing and controlling the attention of the audience. Therefore, one must assume the role of audience while pre-blocking.

Compelling the audience to look at a particular point on the stage is more difficult than getting a television viewer to concentrate on a focal point on his or her home screen. The television director uses close-ups to rivet the home viewer's attention on a person's face, an eye, or a small object held in the hand. However, the stage director deals with a vast expanse of stage space, with an audience made up of people seated close to the apron and those seated in the last row, perhaps 90 feet from the curtain line. The means to magnify a small object or a subtle facial expression to a larger proportion is not available in the theatre. The fringe portions of the setting cannot be masked out completely in order to concentrate on a single element. (Actually, the latter condition can be partially accomplished by turning off all stage lights except one spotlight, which pinpoints a person or an object. This type of focus is often used on the featured singer in a musical, and frequently is employed in plays that are episodic.)

The means available to the director to control attention are complex, but each director learns to refine them into relatively simple procedures. Each composition demands a specific focal point, and each change of composition must carry the appropriate focus throughout transition. A real understanding of *what* commands attention is the common tool of most directors. Actors should possess the same understanding and appreciation so that their work will be profitable and effective.

What commands attention? A male actor, dressed in a dark costume, alone on the stage, even if seated, commands attention. Whatever he does or says should be the sole focal point of the composition. If he rises and moves about the stage he will capture even stronger attention. If he stands, looking at a book held in his outstretched hand, then stares at a portrait hanging on the right-stage wall, the audience will follow his gaze, noticing the book first, then shifting its attention to the painting. If he turns, crosses to a chair, and sits, the audience will follow his movements. The actor here has employed *movement* and *focus* to control attention.

Our eyes instinctively follow movement. It is difficult for the average spectator at a football game to watch the play of the interior linemen. Eyes are on the halfback who is running with the ball. The magician waves a bright handkerchief and our eyes watch the flutter of silk, while the magician quietly prepares the next trick — using the other hand.

Focus, when used to control attention, merely means that we look where others look. A man standing on the sidewalk looking toward the top of a three-story building will cause others to pause and look up. Focus; meaning to "look at" something, is one of the most frequently given stage directions. When two or more actors are onstage at the same time, the attention usually is on the speaker. If it is a dialogue involving three actors, the attention should shift to each speaker in turn. If movement and repositioning is unwarranted, the director insists that the non-speaking actors focus on the speaker. With two actors training their sights on the speaker, the audience's attention also will be directed to the third actor.

With the male actor, alone on the stage and dressed in a dark costume, imagine a second actor, female, entering the scene. The actress crosses to the right of the seated actor and remains standing. She has, or should have, control of audience attention by virtue of her movement and height advantage. A person who is standing generally holds a stronger position than one who is seated. This concept can be extended to include the use of platforms and steps. The actor on the higher level most likely will control attention.

The actress, if she is wearing a brightly colored costume, will have another immediate attention-controlling factor. In contrast to the dark costume of the actor, her costume attracts the eye. Indeed, costumers have to be careful that certain characters are not too distractingly attired, especially if they are not key figures in the play. Still another way of strengthening the female's position is to have the male turn and watch her as she moves toward him. This again is the use of focus.

If the director wants the actor and actress to share the focus, the actor can stand and both can face each other in one-quarter positions; or she can sit beside him, making certain their positions are of equal strength. When the male needs to regain a significant portion of attention, he may move while the female focuses on him.

Positioning is another method of controlling attention. Sometimes it is necessary to close the position of the less important character and open the position of the speaking actor. This maneuver is usually accomplished by *taking stage* or *giving stage*. Taking stage occurs when the more important actor moves upstage a few inches. Giving stage takes place when the less important actor moves downstage a half step or so. In both instances, the upstage actor (the dominant character) opens position and the downstage actor (the focusing agent) closes position slightly (see Fig. 11).

When a third actor enters, the audience's attention shifts to that character for several reasons: curiosity; the actor's movement; focusing by the two actors already onstage; and, noise — the actor probably has a speech to deliver. (Playwrights seldom bring a character onstage without a line to speak.) If the three indulge in dialogue for several minutes, and if attention should shift from one to another, the director will utilize other devices to control attention and maintain interest in the scene.

In all likelihood, a series of triangle arrangements, movement, and contrast will be used. The triangle is an effective device for arranging three characters on stage, provided the equal spacing of characters is avoided (see Fig. 12).

Taking   Sharing   Giving

Fig. 11. Positioning to control attention.

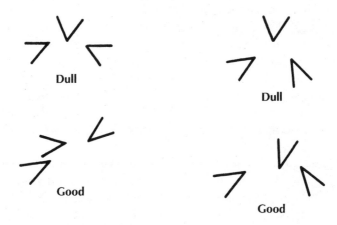

Fig. 12. Triangle arrangements.

The focus can be changed with relatively little movement or compensating activity. If more movement is essential, the director merely alters the shape of the triangle, with the moving actor maintaining control of attention throughout.

Contrast can be an effective device for focus under certain circumstances. For example, if two characters are standing and the third is seated, squatting, kneeling, or in some other different physical attitude, the latter will probably be the center of attention. Contrast as a factor in the control of attention is utilized more effectively, however, when there are four or more characters onstage. Moreover, it can be applied in an additional space relationship, provided the motivation is justifiable. By placing the key character apart from the others, especially if the others are properly grouped, the single character is distinct from the group and commands the eye. (This is illustrated in Fig. 13.) Note that the single figure stands out, even though in a closed position. If this figure were also facing one-half right, he or she would still be dominant because of the space relationship. The group tends to blend together, with no particular point of interest. (It should be pointed out that the stage might appear to be imbalanced, with the force of six characters opposing the force of a single character,

Fig. 13. Using imbalance to distinguish the key character.

but the physical imbalance can be neutralized by what is called emotional balance. The sheer emotional bent of a single character can balance the vast weight and size of a group.)

Two additional considerations of composition deserve brief comment: the need to account for sightlines and the need for variety. Normally, sightlines are thought of in terms of the audience-stage setting relationship. Can the sidewalls be seen from all but the most extreme side seats (as in Fig. 14)? These are important check points for the designer, but in terms of composition the director pre-blocks characters so that they are in full view of the entire audience when they have business, movement, reactions, or lines that are significant. This means that certain characters should not be blocked into masked or semi-masked areas of the stage. They should not be masked by other characters. Sometimes it means they should not be blocked upstage of a bulky piece of furniture or a large set piece.

No formula exists that states how frequently or in what way a composition should be changed. In full-length plays there are hundreds of compositions, each one motivated, each one leading logically into the next, smoothly and without being obvious to an audience. What an audience does notice, however, is the tiring repetition of the same composition and a picture that is obviously posed or held too long. These faults evolve into static staging and audiences soon lose interest. The same response occurs if the director inserts too much action and constant picture changing.

There is, then, a line to draw, and the director's judgment prevails. Some key guidelines are to recognize that the human

Fig. 14. Sightlines.

being cannot focus for very many seconds on a stationary object; that following the repetitious movements of a pendulum can put one to sleep; and that irregular patterns of movement and positioning often lead one to believe that something interesting is about to take place.

The process of play analysis, consultation with other artists of the theatre, and preparation of the prompt book constitute the pre-rehearsal phase of the director's work. It is not unusual at this point for the director to meet with designers to solidify certain ideas and perhaps modify previously made agreements. It also is a prime moment to plan the rehearsal schedule, organize hand property needs, and select and arrange sound and music effects. Once the director begins the rehearsal phase, time becomes increasingly limited. There will be sufficient work to do simply rehearsing and coordinating the work of others. The additional chores of planning and organizing become very burdensome at that time.

Rehearsal

After fulfilling pre-rehearsal preparation, the director enters the rehearsal phase with confidence, knowing more about the play than any other person involved in the production. There is a plan of action, a point of departure. Advance planning will prove beneficial in handling most of the problems that pop up in rehearsals. (However, it is virtually impossible to anticipate *all* the pesky snags that will occur.) The director is a teacher, not only of a play but also of acting — not merely a traffic director of stage movement. An organized director creates an atmosphere in which participants can learn about the craft of acting and the production of good dramatic literature. Directors enter the rehearsal phase knowing that they, too, will learn a great deal more about the play and all other facets of production. Learning is in the involvement, and the director certainly becomes involved.

There are several phases of rehearsal, each demanding a certain number of hours and each having its own function. In the first meeting with the cast (often the other production participants also are invited to the first session), the director establishes the ground rules that the production will follow. It is vital that everyone understand his or her attitude concerning theatre discipline: seriousness of purpose, no horseplay, promptness, quiet, etc. The cast is informed of its responsibility and of its function in the overall production scheme. They should know how the director conducts the phases of rehearsal, what the setting will look like, and what to expect in the way of costumes.

This and subsequent sessions might be devoted to a discussion of the play. Some directors prefer to spend several rehearsal periods analyzing and discussing the script, establishing character relationships, and even delving into specific characterizations and interpretations. Other directors choose to use the first session only for orientation, presenting an overview of the play, and then they begin blocking immediately. Directors determine their own best approach, and it may differ from one play to another, perhaps depending on the nature of the play and the experience of the cast. No two directors work alike, but most directors seek a common goal — a good, meaningful production and an enjoyable learning experience.

Before working with the actors onstage or in the rehearsal

room, the director sees that the floor plan is marked off clearly on the floor and substitute floor properties are set in their proper places. The acting areas, entrances, and the temporary furnishings are explained. Most directors will review stage-direction term-inology and the appropriate shorthand methodology for writing entries into the script. (Actors should habitually carry to each rehearsal, in addition to their script, two sharpened pencils with erasers. If the director pre-blocks and gives the actors their move-ment and composition, they will be expected to write them down. If the actors work out their own blocking, they still will want to write down the comments and suggestions that the director makes.)

Blocking

There are several ways of presenting blocking to the actors. A few directors prefer to give one move at a time, which is the most time-consuming approach and can be particularly irksome to actors because of the frequent interruptions. A less burdensome manner is to give the actors a full page of blocking, have them walk through that portion, then give them another page. Even less time-consuming, and growing in favor among directors, is blocking that is given a scene at a time. What might seem on the surface to be a minor advantage but actually is a strong point is the fact that actors can sit down and write in the blocking more legibly than when they are standing. Also, actors seem to be able to view the space relationships with greater perception if they can look around the stage without, at the moment, moving around it.

Some directors have their assistants write the blocking into all the scripts, copying from the prompt book. This approach may save rehearsal time, but sometimes the process of association is of more value. If actors write in their own blocking, it automatically takes on personal significance.

The number of hours to be expended in blocking rehearsals is relative to the experience of the director and actors, the amount and degree of difficulty of the movement and composition, and the number of rehearsal hours allotted for the total production. As a guidepost, the blocking phase usually requires one-fourth to one-third the total number of rehearsal hours. Directors like to think the blocking is set at that point, but only an inexperienced director believes it. Movement and composition continue to be modified, at least slightly, during the entire course of rehearsals.

Although changes might not be thought of as blocking changes, it is only natural that as actors build their characterizations, as new insights are gained, as actors begin to relate more to one another, some of the original stage directions will be altered.

Both the director and the actors should constantly remember that blocking rehearsals are not intended to produce immediate results. In the heat of concentration, directors sometimes forget the purpose of the rehearsals and strive for depth of characterization or a finished piece of business. This generally brings frustration for both parties. The director fails to get what is wanted; the actors are not yet ready for that stage of character building.

At the same time, actors must heed the director's insistence that they concentrate and derive as much as possible from each session. Blocking is a period of intense cooperation between actors and director. The director needs to see preconceived ideas executed as precisely as possible; otherwise the merits of a plan cannot be determined and changes that need to be made are not detected. Often, after a direction is carried out, the director immediately sees a better way of doing it. Then the adjustment is made, making certain the change is recorded in the prompt book and in the actors' scripts. Nothing in the prompt book is considered sacred except the work of the playwright.

Similarly, the actors' creative contributions may begin to flow *after* the director's initial concepts have been tried. Ideas breed ideas. It is an extremely autocratic director who will not invite suggestions from actors and examine them carefully in the light of the best interests of the play. It is not unusual to discover that a movement created by an actor during rehearsal is more appropriate and better motivated than that invented by the director during pre-blocking.

Finally, haste in establishing the visual patterns and positions may result in misunderstanding and uncertainty in the actors. Overindulgence in pinpoint placement and precise movement may prove overly time-consuming and may impair the spontaneity of subsequent rehearsal phases. (The movement should be permitted to be modified as characterizations are developed.)

Developing Characterizations

When each act is completely blocked and reviewed, actors are ready to commit their lines to memory. The memorization period extends into the next rehearsal phase, when characterization and character relationships are studied, developed, and partially refined. During this phase the director asks for continual, 100 percent involvement, and that additional time — outside of rehearsal — be spent learning lines. By this time, movement and composition should be second nature to the actor. By the end of the characterization phase, lines, movement, and composition should be second nature.

Together, the actors and the director explore ramifications of interpretation, striving to find the most effective delivery of lines that incorporate appropriate motivation and truthfulness of expression. Together they seek insights into characters that are significant and meaningful. Together they examine the infinite possibilities for characterizations — movement, mannerisms, business — and select those that best communicate the author's intent.

During this phase the director and actors are engrossed in continuing cycles of feeding ideas to each other. The actor reaches out for a characterization and may do something that stimulates the director, something that evokes an idea. The director feeds the idea to the actor, who in turn thinks about it, works with it, and creates another spark that ignites the director. The process is called "helping the actor with discovery" by some authorities; others call it stimulus-response. Regardless of terminology, it is the ideal type of creative involvement between actors and director.

Lines must be completely memorized while the characterization development phase is still in progress, because the practice hand properties should be used as soon as possible. The effective use of hand props and the development of good hand and arm gestures are sharply curtailed as long as scripts are held in the hand. Likewise, scenes involving close physical contact cannot be rehearsed properly.

Experimentation, trial and error, and repetition of that which is finally selected are the earmarks of characterization rehearsals. Directors, retaining the role of teacher, try to learn the best way to work with each actor. Some actors need more suggestions than others. Some will develop more slowly than others. Some will be more sensitive to criticism. Not all will possess similar endurance levels. Rarely does a cast reach a common point of development at the same time.

An assistant to the director, following the prompt book, is an indispensable person when actors are at the line-learning stage. The prompter must be a patient individual, diplomatic but firm. The work entails not only following the script but learning to sense the memorization traits of each actor. Naturally, a few mistakes wil be made, but the prompter should try to learn when an actor is deliberately pausing, when pausing to recall a line, and when a prompt is really needed. Under the pressure of so many responsibilities, actors sometimes become incensed if they are too frequently interrupted with prompts.

Directors vary in their prompting procedures. Some permit their actors to signal the need for a prompt by calling "line" or by snapping their fingers. A danger is attached to these approaches because too often the signal becomes a reflex action. If the need for help persists, the actors may be snapping their fingers onstage in the performance — to the distress of the director and the bewilderment of the audience. Actors should establish for themselves a discipline whereby they pause for a moment and try to recall the line before requesting help. Gradually they become less dependent on the prompts; they reach such a point of self-sufficiency that they can cover dropped lines or any other stage emergency.

Another "house rule" concerns the misreading of a line. A director may want the fouled line repaired immediately by having the prompter read the line correctly; or the prompter may be instructed to note the mistake and alert the actor upon completion of the scene. A convenient guideline is to observe the frequency of interruptions during particular rehearsals. During rehearsals, when stoppages are frequent and expected, correcting a misreading is not much of an intrusion, but when actors are working toward a sense of line and action continuity, it is best if their concentration is not disrupted.

Prompts should never be whispered; they should be spoken loudly and clearly. An actor in rehearsal should never have to say "Huh?" to the prompter. During performances, whispered prompts will be heard in the last row, but when they are spoken in a low voice they will not reach the first row. Probably, prompters will not be used during dress rehearsals and performances. Few directors employ them at such times, and it benefits the production if they are not used. It is far more advantageous to train actors to know the play and understand the scenes so well that they can cover for lapses of memory or any other eventuality — the door that fails to open or the telephone bell that fails to ring on cue. Actors who are trained to remain in character, to retain their poise, and to improvise until difficulties are rectified can sustain a scene without alerting the audience to the fact that a problem exists.

At the end of the characterization phase of rehearsal, actors have a feeling of disjointedness, as if they are no longer moored to a common play. In their earnestness to develop a meaningful character, exploring the possibilities of voice, mind, and body, and inventing appropriate business for their roles, they often lose sight of the total scene, act, or the entire play. The best remedy for this completely normal condition is the next rehearsal phase.

Polish

Sufficient time in the total rehearsal schedule must be allotted to polish, because it is during this phase that the cast once again finds its moorings. It re-catches the continuity of the play, re-establishes relationships with one another, and sets the movement, composition, moods, and tempos that will prevail.

Polish rehearsals should permit the cast to run complete scenes or even acts with few, if any, interruptions. The actors need to get the feel of the total picture, to pace themselves, and to build the climaxes. Some problems will need immediate attention, but most can be noted by the director and the assistants and given to the cast after each run-through. Polish rehearsals should include time for complete runs of scenes, then acts, and finally the complete play. The cast needs one complete run of the entire play, absolutely without interruption, before the technical rehearsal.

The director, who has worked hard and has become deeply involved in the proceedings, must now be able to reach back into a personal reserve and withdraw extra funds of objectivity. At this point, directors cannot afford to overindulge in empathic responses to what they see and hear on the stage. They must continue to play the roles of audience, director, and teacher so that they can evaluate the polish rehearsals. Over and above reacting to the believability and meaningfulness of characterizations, they must assess the action and reaction of the players, their effectiveness as an ensemble, the consistency of style, the various moods for various scenes, the timing of all lines and action, the building of peaks and climaxes, the tempo of each scene, audibility, and sightlines.

A scene or two, or a few segments from scenes, may need additional intensification. Sometimes a few moments spent working them over will be sufficient before running the scene again. If a scene should demand a lengthy period of work, it is best to do it at the end of the scheduled rehearsal, or even the next day, rather than interrupt the rehearsal. As best they can, directors avoid disrupting these rehearsals.

Technical Rehearsal

During the weeks of rehearsal, other indispensable people have been working on various facets of the production: scenery, lights, costumes, properties, publicity, box office, make-up, and promotion. The director has maintained running contacts with those responsible for each area and has coordinated completion deadlines so that all are ready for the technical and dress rehearsals.

The technical rehearsal probably has caused more directors to vow never to direct again than any other phase of play production, but this need not be the case. The technical rehearsal is designed to incorporate all technical components with the work of the actors. Some directors attempt to accomplish the Herculean feat by weaving in each component as it is needed—sound, lights, curtain, action—and still give the actors an opportunity to achieve a full-scale dress rehearsal. Frustration occurs because too soon it is time to go home.

The solution to the problem is not necessarily simple but it can help all concerned retain some degree of sanity. It is twofold; plan in advance, and give the cast a break.

Planning in advance means to organize the actual production routine with the technical director, stage manager, and all others who share a major responsibility a week or more before the technical rehearsal. The director establishes with the lighting technicians the troublesome areas, the flexibility needed, the special effects desired, and a cueing system that shows when and how the lighting move is to be made. Sound cues and curtain cues are established. The stage manager is oriented to the manner in which the production is to operate. This includes routines for scene and property changes. Make-up procedures are outlined and dressing-room space is arranged.

If possible, the heads of the crews should attend the final polish rehearsals and follow the play with scripts, observing when their cues come up, and familiarizing themselves with the total production plan. Polish rehearsals provide excellent opportunities for the stage manager to make "dry runs."

By the technical rehearsal date, the costumes should be completed, the lights should be set, scenery completed and mounted, properties in place, the curtain tested, and sound machinery checked out. All systems should be "go."

This being the first time all of the participants have been assembled at the same time and place, the director orients them on subsequent rehearsals and objectives. The responsibilities of each segment are outlined, and the relationship of each to the other is explained. All must clearly understand that the purpose of the rehearsal is to integrate the technical elements into the play, so that all technical cues are synchronized with the action.

Giving the actors a break does not mean that the actors can take the night off. Rather, consideration is given to them in light of the circumstances. They should not expect or be expected to derive a complete, polished rehearsal from the session. They will have too many adjustments to make. Chances are great that it will be the first time they have worked within the framework of the scenery. They will hear new sounds, even if they have been rehearsing regularly on the stage. The lighting will be strange and hot. They will have to get accustomed to the costumes and to the actual hand and floor properties. Moreover, by this time the cast needs relief from having to concentrate fully on sustaining their characterizations. The technical rehearsal, then, can be a blessing in disguise for all.

The procedures for running the technical rehearsal differ among directors. An approach that gives the technicians and actors confidence in their respective roles is essential. Most directors start at the beginning — the opening cue — and proceed chronologically through the play to the final curtain and light cues, making certain that the timing for each is appropriate. To complete the entire play within a reasonable time limit, they may skip huge portions of dialogue that do not include technical cues. They may concentrate on those segments that involve the technical aspects.

The actors must cooperate by executing their movements, compositions, and delivery of lines exactly as they rehearsed them in the final polish rehearsals. Actors cannot slough off or become careless in any manner; otherwise the proper timing of cues can never be determined.

Repetition of many cues will be necessary. The most complicated sequences of cues generally are repeated three or four times, even if they are perfect the first time. The entire process should be orderly. All participants must recognize the problems of the other cast and crew members. The maneuvering of dimmer handles is different under rehearsal conditions; somehow the movement was smoother earlier in the day when a crew member checked out the lights. The sweeping grand entrance of an actress, dressed in a full skirt, is not quite as sweeping as it was in rehearsal, because the actual doorway restricts her movement. All must adapt themselves calmly, patiently, to the new set of circumstances.

If the advanced planning has been effective and if cool heads prevail, a single rehearsal session should be sufficient to synchronize all technical elements. A perfect execution of all cues is always desirable but seldom achieved, and never absolutely necessary. Subsequent dress rehearsals give all participants an opportunity to tighten the controls on their responsibilities.

Dress Rehearsals

Most directors try to schedule three dress rehearsals. Under ideal circumstances, these rehearsals are complete and uninterrupted run-throughs. On each run, actors and crew strive for performance-level achievement, but the first dress rehearsal should be calculated to permit all participants to reinforce the habits established during the technical rehearsal. Hopefully, a few mistakes will be made, because problems uncovered and corrected during dress rehearsals reduce the chance of their occurrence during the performance.

The director's role during dress rehearsal is to check the tempo of each scene and the overall rhythm, the mood and atmosphere, the peaks and the major climax, the characterizations and their relationships, ensemble playing, projection, as well as the sightlines, scenery, costumes, lighting, and make-up. A superhuman effort? Indeed!

Well-trained assistants can be of special help at this time by making notes of what they observe and what the director tells them to write down. At this point, they are acquainted with the production and should know, generally, what the director wants.

A popular device for note-taking that is used by directors is the tape recorder. Many directors sit in the back row and make notes by speaking them into the recorder. Of course, this necessitates a machine that is relatively noiseless, and the director has to be able to speak in low volume. The system breaks down if murmuring and knob-clicking can be heard onstage by the actors.

There are several advantages to this approach. For one thing, directors who write their own notes remove their eyes and attention from the stage for a few moments. Frequently, too, they write only a fragment of response, which may have little or no meaning when they present their comments to the cast after the run. Second, if directors dictate their notes to an assistant, there is the inevitable loss of meaning in the translation; the message sometimes loses its true connotation. Furthermore, there are the unfortunate times when the assistant does not hear and asks to have the message repeated—and two pages of dialogue pass by during the interval. Finally, when the tape is played back at the critique session, the message not only retains its accuracy but is attended by the director's true sentiments and vocal inflections at the moment of utterance.

Ordinarily, comments are given to the cast and the crew immediately after the complete run. If time permits, the director may want to review a few cues or polish a small segment of a scene. All participants need to know what must still be accomplished in terms of readiness for opening night.

The final dress rehearsal should be given over completely to the stage manager, cast, and crew with provisions that the entire rehearsal is in "performance condition." The only justifiable reason for stoppage would be something like an enemy intercontinental ballistic missile that explodes three feet from the stage door (but only if it creates *serious* damage to the scenery).

The critique session that follows the final dress rehearsal is brief; good sleep and rest are far more important. The director is at the point of no return in terms of making major changes. Some directors will cite the specific notes that must be dealt with. Others will merely review the ensemble, pace, concentration, spontaneity, and energy in general terms. Most directors choose to continue the teaching role through production by passing on a few significant notes after each performance. However, after the final dress rehearsal the role as director is completed.

Suggested Activities

1. Select three plays that you determine will require different styles of setting and acting. Prepare justifications for your decisions.

2. Prepare a list of students and faculty in your school that might make a good team of collaborators if you were directing a play. Explain why each person would be effective in his or her particular job.

3. In the three plays you chose for the first activity, identify the theme of the play and write it in a very careful and precise statement. Have your director check it for accuracy.

4. Take one of the three plays you have read and analyze its structure.

5. Using the same material you used for activity 4, study the dialogue. Take several pages from the first act and describe the rhythm and movement that seem to be reflected in the length and psychological nature of the speeches.

6. Using one of the three plays, draw (to scale) a floor plan indicating the major requirements for entrances, exits, windows, and traffic patterns.

7. Prepare a prompt book. Use what you have already done in the above activities. Pre-block at least one act of the play you choose.

8. By preplanning, build some examples of symmetrical and asymmetrical balance. Using students from your class, demonstrate these for the rest of the class. See if they can guess what you have attempted to do with the idea of balance. Do the same with the concept of focus.

9. With a group of two or more onstage, practice "sharing," "taking," and "giving" stage.

10. Using a play you have chosen, prepare a rehearsal schedule.

11. Take a small scene from a play and block it. Then, using some of your friends, give them instructions on what to do to secure your directing objectives.

12. Take a short scene, block it, and direct it two different ways, to demonstrate that you can secure more than one interpretation by your analysis, blocking, movement, balance, and attention and focus skills.

Play Directing Bibliography

Canfield, Curtis. *The Craft of Play Directing.* New York: Holt, Rinehart & Winston, 1963.

Cole, Toby, and Chinoy, Helen K. (eds.). *Directing the Play.* Indianapolis: Bobbs-Merrill, 1953.

Dean, Alexander, and Carra, Lawrence. *Fundamentals of Play Directing.* 4th ed. New York: Holt, Rinehart and Winston, 1980.

Gorchakov, Nikolai M. *Stanislavsky Directs.* Tr. by Miriam Goldina. New York: Funk & Wagnalls, 1954.

Hodge, Francis. *Play Directing.* 3rd ed. Englewood Cliffs: Prentice-Hall, 1988.

Stanislavski, Constantin. *An Actor Prepares.* Tr. by Elizabeth Reynolds Hapgood. New York: Theatre Arts Books, 1936.

————. *Building a Character.* Tr. by Elizabeth Reynolds Hapgood. New York: Theatre Arts Books, 1949.

Staub, August W. *Creating Theatre.* New York: Harper & Row, 1973.

Welker, David. *Theatrical Direction.* Boston: Allyn & Bacon, 1971.

Wills, J. Robert (ed.). *The Director in a Changing Theatre.* Palo Alto, Calif.: Mayfield Publishing Co., 1976.